# BARNES & NOBLE BASICS™

## getting
# Married

by Andrea Rotondo Hospidor

Formerly published as
**I'm getting Married, Now What?!**

**BARNES
& NOBLE**
B O O K S

For information, contact:
Silver Lining Books
122 Fifth Avenue
New York, NY 10011
212-633-4000

# introduction

**Congratulations! You're getting married!** If you're like most of us, this is something you have dreamed about for a long time, and you want your wedding day to be absolutely perfect. A lovely memory to last a lifetime. But all of a sudden it hits you—there's an awful lot to get done! A wedding date to pick, a dress to find, maybe a caterer to test, and a D.J. to audition. Or even if you want a simpler affair, you need to find that perfect beach for the ceremony or a lovely park for an outdoor reception. And no matter what, there will be bills to pay, people to invite—or not invite—and, well, the list goes on and on. But don't panic. That's where **Barnes & Noble Basics** *Getting Married* comes to your rescue. Written by wedding expert Andrea Rotondo Hospidor, it's packed with creative ideas, money-saving and stress-reducing tips, lists of amazing resources, and lots more to help make your wedding day the momentous event it should be.

Barb Chintz
Editorial Director, the **Barnes & Noble Basics**™ series

# table of contents

CHAPTER

# 1

You've said yes. Now what?
You are about to begin an amazing journey from singlehood to coupledom. But
before the wedding fun and frenzy start,
stop and take a moment to think about your future.

# You're
# Getting Married

# great expectations

**What getting married really means**

*Y*ou're getting married. Congratulations! You did it—you said yes to one of life's most spectacular gifts: marriage. All of a sudden, you have a slew of questions about when you'll get married and what type of ceremony you'll have. If you're feeling a little overwhelmed, don't panic. It's normal. After all, you are going from having a private love affair to making a public commitment. That's a big deal. It's what anthropologists call a rite of passage. Your wedding is more than a party celebrating your discovery of the love of your life. It's the crowning ritual that symbolically moves you through this rite of passage.

Rituals involve several steps or stages. There is the planning stage, the preparation stage, and finally, the ceremony itself. If this all sounds too hard to handle, don't fret. There are wedding planners and organizers to help–see page 72. The most important thing is the last stage of the ritual: the transformation of the single you into the married you. It sounds mysterious, but it isn't. All it means is that when your wedding is over, you and your new spouse both see it as a solid start to your new life as a couple.

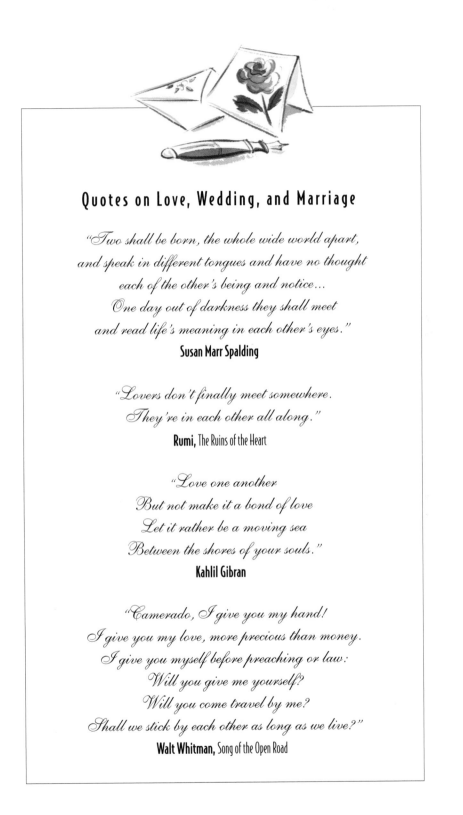

## Quotes on Love, Wedding, and Marriage

*"Two shall be born, the whole wide world apart,
and speak in different tongues and have no thought
each of the other's being and notice...
One day out of darkness they shall meet
and read life's meaning in each other's eyes."*

**Susan Marr Spalding**

*"Lovers don't finally meet somewhere.
They're in each other all along."*

**Rumi,** The Ruins of the Heart

*"Love one another
But not make it a bond of love
Let it rather be a moving sea
Between the shores of your souls."*

**Kahlil Gibran**

*"Camerado, I give you my hand!
I give you my love, more precious than money.
I give you myself before preaching or law:
Will you give me yourself?
Will you come travel by me?
Shall we stick by each other as long as we live?"*

**Walt Whitman,** Song of the Open Road

# now that you've said I will

*I*f dating is about the here and now, marriage is about the future. For many couples, when they get engaged it is the first time they have ever seriously thought about their future. This is why marriage experts suggest that you use the engagement period to reexamine how you and your beloved want your future to unfold. This is especially important if you come from different backgrounds.

The future is something the two of you will create together. It's a lot like building a house, but instead of rooms, you will build shared values and goals. So before you get caught up in the hoopla and planning of your wedding, take some time to review how you both feel about some of the big things in life: work, family, education, faith, money, home, charity. Anything and everything.

## Important Topics to Discuss

- What do we want out of life?

- What type of job or career is each of us working toward?

- Will we change our names to reflect our new married status?

- How much money do we need to live on?
  How much money do we want to live on?

- Where should we live?

- Will we want to live in our own home in the suburbs someday
  or would we prefer an apartment in the city?

- Will we live near our families or not?

- If our religions are different, will one of us convert?

- Do we want to have children? When? How many?

- If our religions are different, which religion will the children be brought up in?

- How will we take care of our children? Day care?
  Will one of us be a stay-at-home parent? Both of us, in some combination?

# ASK THE EXPERTS

**I hear there is something called premarriage counseling. What is that?**

A number of states will waive the **waiting period** and/or give a couple a discount on their marriage license if they go for "premarital counseling." (The waiting period, which can range from none to five days, depending on the state in which you're getting married, is designed to give the engaged parties time to back out, should they want to.) The hope is that such counseling will help decrease the divorce rate by teaching couples how to work through the problems they will inevitably encounter while married. Ideally, the sessions help couples effectively communicate their expectations of marriage and show them how to handle disagreements. Most churches and synagogues offer premarital counseling. In fact, the Roman Catholic Church requires engaged couples to take part in at least eight hours of counseling, or Pre-Cana (see page 81) before they marry. If you aren't a member of a church or synagogue but are interested in counseling, look for a premarital counselor in the Yellow Pages or get help online at MarriageBuilders.com or by calling 651-762-8570.

**Help! The more my fiancé and I talk, the farther apart we seem to be on all the major issues. What should I do?**

Don't panic. This is exactly what an engagement period is supposed to do: root out any major obstacles that could spell heartache once you are married. If there are too many unresolved problems, either postpone the wedding or break your engagement. Do not allow yourself to get caught up in the chaos and expectations of a wedding without first being sure that getting married to your fiancé is what you really want to do.

# blended families

*T*oday's "global village" means that your chances of entering into a **blended family** are high. What does this mean? Well, the term can denote many situations. The most common scenario is that of a second marriage into which children from a previous relationship are brought: hers, his, and ours. The challenge is to create a new family in which everyone feels accepted.

The phrase blended family is also used to describe couples of different faiths who come together in marriage—bridging the gap between Judaic and Christian beliefs, for instance. Ideally, these couples need to decide how their different faiths will be incorporated into their marriage. Often, it is the planning of the wedding that first brings the reality of their different religions front and center. If you and your fiancé are of different faiths, take this time to learn about each other's religion. Attend each other's religious services, learn about the major holidays.

Another type of blended family is the cross-cultural one; for example, a marriage between an African-American and a Japanese-American. Significant cultural and ethnic differences may make it that much more difficult for the couple's families to "blend" together. Ideally, coming together in a marriage means more than just two becoming one. It's about two entire families learning to embrace each other, and when this includes two different cultures, the blending can become more complex. Again, take the time to learn about each other's different cultural and ethnic backgrounds.

## ASK THE EXPERTS

**I am a lapsed Catholic and my fiancé is a nonpracticing Jew. We don't really care about religion, and we were considering getting married by a justice of the peace, but my parents are very religious and we're worried that it might offend them. What should we do?**

Your wedding isn't just about you and your beloved; it's also about your families. Don't be surprised if your parents insist on incorporating their own religious values into the ceremony, especially if they are helping you pay for the wedding. It is up to you either to go along with their requests or to say no gracefully. Talk with your parents and find out exactly which religious ritual or prayer is most critical to them, then decide if there is a way to incorporate this into your wedding. One creative solution: You can have a justice of the peace perform the ceremony but also have a rabbi and priest read certain key ceremony passages.

## FIRST PERSON DISASTER STORY

### Translation Woes

Many members of my husband's extended family flew over from Korea for our wedding in New York City. He hadn't seen them in years and was thrilled that they'd made the trip. The only problem was that none of them spoke English. At the reception, my new husband served as a translator, introducing them to our friends and my family. I wish that I'd hired a translator so that he could have had a chance to eat and relax a bit.

**Christy M., New York, New York**

# money and marriage

## Terms of your engagement

$\mathscr{P}$lanning a wedding is often the first time couples encounter the Big Bad Boogie Monster known as the wedding budget. Weddings can be expensive, and you'll see each other's spending style up front. Chances are, you and your intended have the same philosophy about saving and spending money. If not, this is the time to air your differences. Don't panic: a difference of opinion about spending and saving money is normal in a marriage. The happy couple is one that knows each other's habits and has worked out a system to accommodate them.

It's a good idea to take some time to figure out how you both feel about money. Consider this: Do you both hope to make a lot of money? If one of you makes less than the other, is that okay?

Next, look at each other's concrete spending and saving habits. For starters, consider how you handle credit card bills. Do you pay each bill in its entirety as soon as you get it? Or do you pay just the minimum that is due? Do either of you ever not pay a bill and just let it ride for a month? What about other debts you may have incurred— for example, college loans? Do you pay your portion regularly and on time? Have either of you ever borrowed money from siblings, parents, or other relatives? Some people think it's perfectly fine to borrow money from friends but not relatives. Others feel that such matters should be strictly business and will only borrow from a bank or get money through a credit card cash advance. How do you feel about borrowing money?

Now look at each other's saving habits. Have you or your beloved put any money into an IRA or a 401(k)? Do you think you can create a realistic savings plan for long-term goals such as a house or your retirement?

# ASK THE EXPERTS

**My mom suggested I get a credit report on my fiancé. I was shocked and told her that it wouldn't tell me anything I didn't know about him already.**

Once you are married, you become legally liable for the debts your spouse incurs. That's why it's so important to talk about money before you marry and to review your feelings about it, as well as to discuss any past money problems you may have had. A credit report will tell you all about your fiancé's credit history—in other words, how much debt he has taken on and how well he has paid it back. If he has paid his debts in a timely fashion, he will have a good report. If there are delinquencies, liens against properties for nonpayment or bankruptcies, they will show up on a credit report and reveal a poor rating. If your intended has had trouble with money in the past, it may not be a bad thing, provided he is working toward improving his credit history with a sound repayment schedule. Whatever you do, don't obtain a credit report behind his back. Talk about any concerns openly.

**This is my second marriage, and I have two children from a previous relationship. Should I get a prenuptial agreement?**

A prenuptial agreement is a great way to protect your children's assets. With a prenup, your spouse will waive his or her rights to any specified property or assets upon your death or divorce. Your children will then receive the money and property you originally intended for them. A will instructing that your assets be distributed among your children may not be enough, because in certain states the surviving spouse is entitled to a portion of the inheritance unless a previous legal agreement has been processed. If you don't wish to get a prenuptial agreement, you can set up a trust to protect your children's assets. See an estate lawyer.

## A Prenuptial Agreement

A prenuptial agreement is a legal contract that spells out the rights of each person with regard to the property of the other in the event of divorce or death. It is a wise idea if either of you has children from another relationship or is coming to the marriage with a lot of money or assets (such as property or a business).

# now what do I do?

## Answers to common questions

**I want a big wedding, but my fiancé wants to get married right away. If we do that, we won't have enough money for a lavish affair. How can we both get what we want?**

A small wedding versus a big one; now versus later. Those are big differences of opinion. Obviously, you need to sit down and really talk this out. Ask your fiancé whether he wants to get married right away in order to save money or to avoid making a private commitment so publicly. Explain why a big wedding is important to you. Look for alternative locations that would be inexpensive but elegant, like having the ceremony in a local park followed by a reception in your parents' house. Inquire about weekday discounts at area hotels and country clubs. Get married in the morning and host a buffet brunch instead of a sit-down meal. Forgo full bouquets and have each of your bridesmaids carry a single bloom. For the gospel on saving money on weddings, pick up a copy of Denise and Alan Fields' *Bridal Bargains*.

**I don't think I can handle a big wedding. Can't we just elope?**

Planning a wedding is a challenge. Most people are glad they took it on, but it's not for everyone. An **elopement** is often a civil ceremony that involves going to a justice of the peace (see page 50). Usually, the officiant has witnesses on hand to sign your marriage certificate. Once you get your license to marry (see page 90), you can elope in a matter of minutes or days depending on the state. You can also personalize your elopement (see page 50-51 for some hassle-free ideas).

**What exactly do you learn in premarital counseling?**

Essentially, you and your intended learn how to resolve conflicts by effective communiation. When most couples fight, they resort to: shouting, withdrawing, blaming, refusing to listen, or avoidance of the problem by changing the subject. In order to resolve conflicts, you each need to learn how to talk through heated issues. That means letting each of you talk out your feelings without interruption, then each mirroring back what you heard to make sure you understood it correctly. Another technique is to use sentences beginning with "I" instead of "You," as in "I feel really hurt when you don't listen," as opposed to "You never listen to me" or "You're so selfish."

**I am Catholic and my boyfriend is Jewish. When we were dating, this didn't seem to be a big deal. Now that we're engaged, shouldn't one of us think about converting?**

That depends on how important your religion is to you and the role you expect it to play in your marriage. One of the great things about being engaged is that you have time to work through these big issues and to reconsider your feelings. Ask yourselves: Are you both content to have an interfaith marriage? Now ask yourselves: If you have children, will the children be brought up with one or both religions in their lives? If one of you decides to convert before you marry, be aware that it will take time. You may have to postpone your wedding.

## OW WHERE DO I GO?!

### CONTACTS

*Bride's*

**www.brides.com**
One of the grand dame magazines dedicated to the bride and groom of the 21st century.

*Elegant Bride*

**www.elegantbride.com**
A great magazine resource offering elegant ideas for your wedding day. Lots of real wedding reviews are included.

*Modern Bride*

**www.modernbride.com**
Terrific magazine redefining modern-day wedding traditions.

**www.theknot.com**
Check out this Web site for a wealth of information on planning a wedding. An extensive message board, online chat rooms, and a gift registry make The Knot the place to go for the bride-to-be.

### BOOKS

**The RoMANtic's Guide: Hundreds of Creative Tips for a Lifetime of Love**
by Michael Webb

**How to Write Your Own Premarital Agreement: With Forms**
by Edward A. Haman

**Celebrating Our Differences: Living Two Faiths in One Marriage**
by Mary Helene Rosenbaum

**Complete Idiot's Guide to Interfaith Relationships**
by Laurie E. Rozakis

**Guess Who's Coming to Dinner: Celebrating Interethnic, Interfaith, and Interracial Relationships**
by Brenda Lane Richardson

# 2

Get ready! It's time to spread the word and start thinking about
the type of wedding you want. It's also time to have an engagement party.
Remember, it's your party, and you can have fun if you want to.

Mr. and Mrs. Andrew Colgate
of Dartmouth, Massachusetts,
announce the engagement
of their daughter,

Kimberly Ann,
to
Kevin Henry Taylor,

son of
Mr. and Mrs. Adam Taylor
of Hampton Creek,
New Hampshire.

A June wedding is planned.

# guess what?

**Here comes the bride**

$\mathcal{A}$ big test for you as an engaged couple comes when you announce your plans to your families. While you may think you know exactly what your parents and siblings will say, brace yourself for any deviations from the plan. The rule of thumb here is: Expect the unexpected.

Most often, parents are thrilled when they find out that their child has found his or her soul mate. However, family relationships can be complicated, and this development signals a change in the family structure. It may take some parents a little time to get used to the idea that their "baby" is about to get married.

The situation may be made even more complicated if your family doesn't know your fiancé very well. Make every effort to have him or her spend some time with your parents and siblings. This should ease any minor misgivings family members may have about your impending nuptials. And remember, you're not just marrying your fiancé, you're marrying his family, too. Get to know them.

And be prepared for a million questions! Although you've probably only been engaged a short time—maybe even a few hours—people will expect you to have already tackled life's big questions. When are you getting married? Are you going to have children? Will you move away? Not to mention, who will be your maid of honor? Just smile and say, "We're so happy to be engaged. We'll start making plans soon."

 # ASK THE EXPERTS

**We just got engaged, and I want to call and tell our families, but my fiancé thinks we should wait and tell them in person. We live 10 hours away from them and probably won't be able to visit for another month or so. What's the best thing to do?**

Good news is good news whether it's delivered over the phone or in person. So why wait? Pick up the phone and call them. Most parents are sure to feel hurt if they're left out of such good news. Your next visit will still be exciting because you will be engaged.

**My fiancé and I are about to announce our engagement to his family. I'm worried that his three sisters will want to be in the wedding party, and I'm not sure that I want to include them. What should I say if they ask?**

The best solution is to agree beforehand not to discuss any actual wedding plans. Again, when asked about specifics simply say, "We haven't decided on anything yet. For now, we just want to share our good news."

**I'm divorced. Should I tell my ex-husband that I'm remarrying?**

If you are still in contact with your ex, then it's important to notify him sooner rather than later. It's better if he hears the news from you instead of from other family members or your children. If you are no longer in contact, then there is no need to bring him up to date on your life.

# your dream wedding

What event style is in your mind's eye?

*Y*ou've gone public with the good news, and now the fun begins. What kind of wedding do you want? Your budget (see chapter 4) will determine certain aspects of your event, such as the location and the menu you choose. The style of your wedding, however, is up to you. Here is a list of styles to choose from—feel free to mix and match.

## Dream A Little Dream

Below are some sample wedding styles—just to give you ideas.

| | Dress | Wedding Party | Ceremony Location | Reception Location | |
|---|---|---|---|---|---|
| **Traditional Formal or Semiformal Wedding** | Floor-length white gown and cathedral train | Maid of honor, bridesmaids, best man, ushers, flower girl, ring bearer | Bride's house of worship | Hotel, country club, or reception hall | |
| **Intimate Wedding** | Tea-length ivory dress or suit | Maid of honor, best man | Public garden | Private room in hotel or your favorite restaurant | |
| **Destination Wedding** | Traditional Polynesian wedding gown | Any combination of bridesmaids and ushers | Hawaiian beach | Beach or resort patio | |
| **Theme Wedding** | Medieval gown | Any combination of bridesmaids and ushers (also wearing theme attire) | Mansion or castle grounds | Mansion or castle dining room | |
| **Ethnic Wedding** | Traditional ethnic dress (in China, women wear gorgeous red dresses during the ceremony) | Any combination of bridesmaids and ushers (wearing traditional or ethnic attire) | Traditional house of worship | Hotel, country club, reception hall, or private room in your favorite restaurant | |
| **Elopement** | White suit or casual dress | None (witnesses can be provided by officiant) | Town hall or Las Vegas chapel | Dinner at an elegant restaurant | |

| Guest List | Menu | Planning Assistance From | Engagement Period |
|---|---|---|---|
| 100 plus | Salad, chicken cordon bleu | Professional wedding planner, mother of the bride, and friends | 12-16 months |
| 2-20 | Asian dim sum | Mother of the bride and friends | 6-8 months |
| Any number | Luau style | Destination wedding planner, resort, or travel specialist | 8-12 months |
| Any number | A feast of game meats and seasonal vegetables | Professional wedding planner | 8-12 months |
| Any number | Ethnic foods (Italian weddings offer a dessert table in addition to wedding cake) | Draw upon the knowledge of your family members or your officiant | 8-12 months |
| None | Anything you wish | Do it yourself or your officiant | Usually quite short |

# hear ye! hear ye!

**An announcement befitting the occasion**

*O*nce you've told your family about your engagement, it's time to let all your friends and colleagues know. You can accomplish this task by making phone calls, placing an announcement in the newspaper, or throwing an engagement party (more on that later in this chapter). Traditionally, newspaper announcements are handled by the bride's parents. However, feel free to call the newspapers yourselves, if you like. This is especially true if this is a second marriage for either of you or if you are marrying later in life and have been living on your own for many years.

## Karen Adams, Daniel Williams

James and Linda Adams of Bethesda, MD, have announced the engagement of their daughter, Karen Jeannine Adams, to Daniel Martin Williams.

Ms. Adams is an assistant buyer with Lindston department store in Bethesda. She graduated from Northeastern University, where she majored in psychology.

Mr. Williams, a native Washingtonian, is a systems analyst with Reddington Pharmaceuticals. He graduated cum laude from George Mason University, receiving a degree in computer science.

The couple plan to wed in September at United Methodist Church in Washington, DC, followed by a honeymoon trip to the Bahamas.

An example of an engagement announcement in the newspaper.

# ASK THE EXPERTS

**How do we submit an engagement announcement to our local newspaper?**

Most newspapers print engagement announcements. You may wish to contact your local paper as well as the newspapers in your parents' hometowns. Many papers request that you fill out a form they've designed especially for this occasion. If they don't have an official form, follow the one below. And don't forget to send announcements to the alumni newsletters and/or alumni magazines of your alma maters. Announcements should be sent no more than one year in advance—and no later than six weeks before—your wedding day.

Bride's Name: _____

Bride's College: _____ Major: _____ Yr. of Graduation: _____

Bride's Employer: _____ Title: _____

Groom's Name: _____

Groom's College: _____ Major: _____ Yr. of Graduation: _____

Groom's Employer: _____ Title: _____

Month/Season of Wedding: _____

Location of Wedding: _____

Bride's Parents' Names: _____

Bride's Parents' Hometown: _____

Groom's Parents' Names: _____

Groom's Parents' Hometown: _____

# choosing the wedding party

**Decisions, decisions**

*C*hoosing your **wedding party**—those loved ones who will stand beside you and your beloved during the ceremony—can be a bit tricky. First, don't make any decisions until you and your fiancé have determined the size and style of your wedding.

Before choosing the members of your wedding party, think about what you're asking them to do. For example, a **maid** or **matron of honor** should be someone who has the time and energy to help you with wedding planning. Ideally, she should also be someone you can confide in—someone who will give you honest opinions on everything from dress styles to reception halls. **Bridesmaids** are close friends you want to help you with your wedding. **Junior bridesmaids** are younger siblings or close relatives ages 7 through 15. **Honor attendants** or **greeters** are friends and family members to whom you give select jobs, such as doing a reading at the ceremony, greeting guests, or manning the guest book at the reception.

## FIRST PERSON DISASTER STORY

### My Bumbling Maid of Honor

I asked my college roommate to be my maid of honor. She went shopping with me for my dress, but she wasn't helpful because she liked them all. When we looked for her dress, she couldn't decide on anything so I had to choose for her. Finally, after dropping hints about my bridal shower and seeing her puzzled face, I got really mad. Then I realized she didn't know what was expected of her, and I apologized. I got some books about weddings, and we both read them. It felt like old times at school. She cohosted my shower and did all these sweet things that made it special. At the wedding, she was the only one who knew how to put us in the right order for the receiving line!

**Kerry H., Elkhart, Indiana**

# ASK THE EXPERTS

**I asked my sister to be my maid of honor, and she seemed excited at first, but now she seems uninterested. What's going on?**

She's probably happy to be taking part in your special occasion, but she may feel that your impending marriage means you'll be leaving her behind. She may even just be caught up in her own life and doesn't realize she isn't there for you. Or she may not know what to do. Try discussing it with her. She may not realize how much you need her.

**I showed my maid of honor the gown I chose for my attendants, and when she saw the price tag, she told me she couldn't be in my wedding party. Shouldn't she buy the gown no matter how much it costs?**

Not necessarily. If your friend can't afford the gown and you have your heart set on it, offer to partially pay for it or give the dress to her as a gift. If you can't afford it either, consider selecting something less expensive.

**My fiancé's best friend is a woman. Can she be his "best man"?**

Absolutely! She can wear the same style of dress that your bridesmaids wear, or she can choose one that complements theirs. She will handle all the usual duties, including arranging a tux fitting for the ushers and scheduling the bachelor party. In this case, it will probably be a low-key event at a restaurant or favorite bar. Oftentimes, a **Jack and Jill party** (a co-ed bachelor/bachelorette party) is hosted, and the entire wedding party goes out together with the bride and groom.

## Who's in the Wedding?

**Maid of Honor:** She will be your right-hand helper. She will go gown shopping with you, and will help with the myriad decisions. She will also coordinate a bridal shower (if you wish) and bachelorette party and act as your on-site therapist.

**Bridesmaids:** Your bridesmaids will also help with decorations, spread the word about your gift-registry options and attend your bridal shower and bachelorette party.

**Flower Girl (optional):** She'll walk down the aisle right before you do, scattering flower petals along the way.

**Best Man:** He'll be your fiancé's right-hand man during the planning process. He'll corral the ushers and will coordinate tuxedo fittings.

**Ushers/Greeters:** The ushers (men) or greeters (women) will seat wedding guests, pass out ceremony programs and oftentimes will accompany a bridesmaid down the aisle. A rule of thumb: one usher per 30 guests.

**Ring Bearer (optional):** He carries the wedding rings to the couple during the ceremony.

# gift registries

## The etiquette of asking

*W*hile the idea of registering for gifts at various stores may make you uncomfortable at first, your guests expect it. In fact, most friends and family will expect you to set up a registry soon after you become engaged and have set a date, so don't put it off.

Be sure to register for items in all price ranges. This will allow your guests to make an appropriate selection within their budgets. For convenience, include some stores that allow people to shop online or by phone.

While most people prefer to give "stuff" to newlyweds, you can request items to enhance your honeymoon, such as a romantic dinner, scuba-diving lessons, airfare contributions, and hotel or resort accommodations. These three companies specialize in honeymoon and romance travel: Beverly Clark Travel (**www.beverlyclarktravel.com**), Honeyluna (**www.honeyluna.com**), and After I Do (**www.afterIdo.com**).

It's unusual, but some couples prefer to forego gifts and register instead for help purchasing a new home. Check out PNC Bank's MatriMoney Wedding Registry (call 888-762-2265 for information). Your guests' contributions will go toward a down payment on a new home. Charity registrations can also be arranged online with your favorite charitable organization, or they can supply you with donation cards to be included with your invitations.

# the engagement party

**Where, when, and how much?**

*T*raditionally, the **engagement party** is hosted by the bride's family, and the guest list consists of close friends and family. But that was in the old days. Nowadays, most couples throw their own engagement party or "couples shower."

Whatever you do, don't add the following line to your party invitations: "We are registered at..." It's considered crass. Instead, tell your family and close friends where you have registered and let them spread the word. The only instance where it's okay to ask for something specific is if you are requesting donations to a charity in lieu of gifts. Then go ahead and print a line about your wishes on your party invitations. For those wishing to forego gifts altogether, invite guests to a party but keep the good news a secret until everyone arrives. It's also acceptable to print "No gifts, please" on your invitations. Even so, guests usually come bearing presents, so have a table ready for them.

If your family wasn't thrilled by the news of your wedding plans, skipping the engagement party may be a good idea. However, why not invite both families to a neutral location, such as a tearoom or wine bar? Let them spend a few hours getting to know each other—it may open the door to important family discussions.

 # ASK THE EXPERTS

**Whom should we invite to our engagement party?**

Wedding etiquette dictates that whomever is invited to the engagement party should also be invited to the wedding. Think about it: If they attend the engagement party but not the wedding, chances are they will feel hurt and left out, or worse, they'll think they did something awful for you to have crossed them off your list. If your wedding reception site turns out to be too small to accommodate all of the people you invited to your engagement party, then it's best to find an alternate reception site that can manage your entire guest list. If that isn't possible, be sure to tell your guests at the engagement party that you are having a very private wedding with just family.

**Who is expected to pay for the engagement party?**

An engagement party is not a necessity, but it is an additional way to celebrate if time and finances permit. Generally, the bride's parents foot the bill, and often the event is held in their home. However, it's perfectly okay if the groom's parents contribute or if the couple themselves throw the party. The important thing is to have your family and friends gathered around you for this special occasion. There's nothing wrong with having a low-key event featuring pizza or a few deli trays.

# now what do I do?

## Answers to common questions

**We got engaged a few weeks ago, and already my mom has gone on reception-hall inspections without me! She's contacted caterers, florists, and photographers. It's great that she wants to help, but it seems like she's already decided how our wedding is going to be. What should I do?**

First of all, rejoice that you have a mom who is so excited about your big day! She probably feels that she should jump in and do everything she can to make your wedding perfect. Explain to her how much you appreciate her help and enthusiasm. Then, methodically detail your vision of the wedding. Here's a big lesson for brides: Delegate those tasks you'd like help with, then firmly but gently tell her what you would like to control yourself. Once some basic guidelines are established, you'll both feel better.

**My fiancé and I are very lucky to be on solid financial footing, and we don't want our family or friends to buy us engagement or wedding gifts. Instead, we'd like them to donate to the charity of our choice. Is that okay?**

It's more than okay; it's wonderful! Discuss which charity you'd like to honor, then give them a call. Explain what you're doing and ask how donations should be handled. Then include a card with your engagement party and wedding invitations explaining that instead of gifts, you'd like donations to be made to this charity. You will probably still receive a few small gifts, but you'll be happy knowing that your friends and family have helped a worthy cause.

**I am Greek-American and my fiancé is an all-American Southern man. Can we incorporate multiple customs into our wedding celebration?**

Making a connection between your two cultures is a great way to personalize your ceremony and reception. There's no reason you can't combine customs from the South and traditions from Greece. Ask family members about customs they remember, then search the library and Internet for more ideas.

# OW WHERE DO I GO?!

## CONTACTS

**Bridesmaid Aid**
www.bridesmaidaid.com
Want to know how women really feel about being bridesmaids? This cheeky guide will help your sisters or girlfriends become dutiful attendants *and* have the time of their lives at your wedding.

## GIFT REGISTRIES

**Bloomingdale's**
www.bloomingdales.weddingchannel.com

**Crate & Barrel**
www.crateandbarrel.com

**Home Depot**
www.homedepot.com

**JCPenney**
www.jcpenney.com

**The Knot**
www.theknot.com

**Macy's**
www.macysweddingchannel.com

**Pier 1 Imports**
www.pierone.com

**Tiffany & Co.**
www.tiffany.com

**Williams-Sonoma**
www.williams-sonoma.com

## BOOKS

**The Best Man's Handbook: A Guy's Guide to the Big Event**
by Jim Grace

**I Need to Do What?! A Wedding Guide for the Groom, Best Man, & Ushers**
by G.C. Van Deusen

**The Bridesmaid's Survival Guide: A Hilarious Handbook to Womanhood's Most Dubious Distinction**
by Mary Kay McDermott

**I'm in the Wedding Too: A Complete Guide for Flower Girls & Junior Bridesmaids**
by Caroline Plaisted

*Esquire's* **Things a Man Should Know About Marriage: A Groom's Guide to the Wedding and Beyond**
by Scott Omelianuk and Ted Allen

**The Bridal Party Handbook: A Complete Guidebook for All Members of the Bridal Party**
by Sharon Naylor

# 3

There are so many great ways to tie the knot!
It's time to decide which wedding style suits you. Go for a traditional affair,
or marry barefoot on a beach. The possibilities are endless!

# Wedding Style

# wedding wishes

**Determine
your style**

*M*ost brides-to-be spend a lot of time dreaming about what their wedding day will be like. Will you walk down the aisle of a city cathedral or toss your bouquet from the heights of a hot air balloon? Or both? Those wedding dreams should help reveal your **wedding style**. Now it's time to determine how those dreams can become a reality. Of course, how much money you have to spend will directly influence your location choice, menu options, and vendor selections. (See chapter 4 for an in-depth budget discussion.)

If you marry locally, the resources in your region will also play a role. Consider incorporating area customs or resources. For example, a couple in Maine married in a clearing in the woods and held their reception at an old hunting lodge. For **favors** (the small gifts the bride and groom give to guests), they gave locally made maple syrup.

What's the most important factor in determining your wedding style? Your imagination! Review the questions on the next page to help you figure out which wedding is right for you and your fiancé. Most weddings are a mix of the old and new. Feel free to create your own style.

## FIRST PERSON      DISASTER STORY

### Not Our Style

**W**hen I think back on our wedding day, I cringe! I kept telling my parents that we didn't want a large wedding, but they insisted on inviting extended family, friends, and colleagues from work. We didn't eat a morsel at the reception, and because there were so many guests to greet, we barely had time to spend with our true friends and close family members. I should have put my foot down or at least made a compromise. It was our wedding day, and we didn't even enjoy it.

**Susan Z., Cincinnati, Ohio**

# ASK THE EXPERTS

**How do we know which type of wedding is right for us?**

Traditional, ethnic, intimate, destination, exotic destination, elopements, and theme weddings are the standard options. Each of these will be discussed in depth later in this chapter. For now, ask yourself the following questions. The answers should help you determine your wedding style.

**1.** Do you both enjoy being the center of attention?

**2.** Do you have a large family and a lot of friends?

**3.** Are you a traditionalist, or will you throw out the conventional in exchange for something new and quirky?

**4.** Is this a second marriage for either of you?

**5.** Would you prefer to celebrate in a quiet way with just the two of you?

**6.** Are you planning to wear an ornate white wedding gown with a cathedral-length train?

**7.** Do you picture a large wedding party or just a maid of honor and best man?

**8.** What is your wedding-day budget?

**9.** Would you prefer an indoor or outdoor ceremony?

**10.** Will any children from previous relationships be included in your ceremony?

# traditional weddings

**Something old, something new, something borrowed, something blue**

*L*et's face it: There is something very comforting about tradition. Following in the footsteps of your parents, grandparents, and great-grandparents can be very rewarding. If you're the sentimental type, you may consider marrying in the church or synagogue you attended while growing up, wearing your mother's or grandmother's wedding gown, and hosting a reception complete with a bouquet toss.

A **traditional wedding** can mean many things. Generally, it signifies that your parents will play a large role in your wedding and will have some say in the guest list, inviting extended family and old family friends. A church or synagogue ceremony is common, followed by a reception at a hotel, country club, or function hall. The wedding party includes a maid of honor, several bridesmaids, a best man, and additional ushers. While a traditional wedding may seem old hat, you can personalize it to your individual tastes.

# ASK THE EXPERTS

**How can we personalize our traditional wedding?**

1. Write your own vows, or ask your officiant (the official who marries you) to personalize the vows he customarily uses.

2. Don't limit yourselves to often-used ceremony readings. Consider poems, passages from books and song lyrics.

3. Don't be afraid to drop customs you don't like, such as the garter toss.

4. Incorporate a different closure into your wedding ceremony. Don't have your guests throw rice (which is harmful to birds if swallowed); instead have your guests throw rose petals. If there will be young children at your wedding, have them blow bubbles as you exit.

5. Instead of hiring limousines, rent a fleet of fun cars, such as Volkswagen Beetles.

6. Forego the usual first dance and have an anniversary dance in which the master of ceremonies will ask all married couples to hit the dance floor. Then have him ask those who have been married less than an hour to sit down, those who have been married less than one year, five years, etc. In the end, the couple married the longest will remain dancing.

7. For food, try something different, such as Asian dim sum, pasta, and carving stations or an old-fashioned turkey dinner with all the trimmings.

8. In addition to your wedding photographer, have a friend take Polaroids of guests during the reception and dinner. Have another friend assemble the photos in inexpensive paper frames, and after the cake cutting, you and your groom can personally deliver these photo gifts to each table.

# ethnic traditions

*E*very nationality has its own unique traditions and customs when it comes to weddings. The symbolism speaks volumes when you include some of these elements in your modern-day nuptials. There is also nothing wrong with adopting a custom from another ethnic group if the meaning touches you. Here are some examples:

**African-American:** Consider walking down the aisle to the beat of **African drummers**. Their presence is significant because during the days of slavery, it was illegal for a person of African descent to play them. (It was thought to be a form of covert communication between slaves.) If the use of drums during the processional is too much for you, consider using them during the recessional only. **Jumping the broom** is another well-known custom. Slaves were not allowed to marry, so couples improvised. They would jump over a broom together, symbolizing their leap into a new life as one. Today, couples sometimes decorate the broom, which becomes a wonderful keepsake to be displayed in the couple's home and to be passed down to their children.

**Irish:** The **Claddah ring** (an engagement ring featuring an elaborate design that resembles a crown) is a recognized symbol of love and loyalty throughout the world, but it originated in Claddah, a fishing village in Galway, Ireland. The crown faces inward, toward the wrist, when a woman gets engaged. During the ceremony, the direction of the ring is changed so that the crown faces the fingertips. This shows the world your commitment as a married couple.

**Spanish:** Brides in Spain forego the white wedding dress and instead select a black gown. While it may seem a bit odd, it signifies that the bride's commitment will not end until death. Touches of red are also common.

**Greek Orthodox:** During the traditional ceremony, the couple is crowned with floral wreaths as a sign of honor. Wedding bands are worn on the right hand instead of the left.

**Chinese:** A tea ceremony is a beautiful, solemn event that is incorporated into Chinese weddings. The bride offers a cup of tea to the groom's family, while he brings his offering (anything from jewelry to money) to her side of the family. Each family member sips the tea and then gives the couple a **hong boa** (a red parcel containing money or jewelry for the bride and groom).

**Japanese:** Similar to the Chinese tea ceremony is the Japanese **sharing of sake** called the **san-san-kudo**. At the end of the ceremony, the bride, groom, and their parents each take a sip of sake from each of the three cups. This symbolizes the new bond of the families.

## Now Where Do I Go?!

**ASIAN WEDDING TRADITIONS**
**Wild Geese and Tea: An Asian-American Wedding Planner** by Shu Shu Costa

**AFRICAN-AMERICAN TRADITIONS**
**The Nubian Wedding Book** by Ingrid Sturgis
**African-American Wedding Readings** by Tamara Nikuradse
**African-American Wedding Manual** by Rev. Willie F. Wilson
**Jumping the Broom: The African-American Wedding Planner** by Harriette Cole

Great online source:
The African Wedding Guide at **www.melanet.com/awg**

# intimate weddings

**Just your nearest
and dearest**

$\mathcal{M}$any couples consider hosting an **intimate wedding**—one in which the guest list is rather small (usually fewer than 20 people). For some, the very idea of marrying in public is counter to their belief that the joining of their souls should be a very private moment, shared only by those closest to their hearts. Other couples are simply shy and would not enjoy a large-scale wedding with 100 pairs of eyes staring at them all day long. And finally, others find hosting an intimate wedding to be a very cost-effective method of marrying.

Is an intimate wedding right for you and your fiancé? Draw up a rough guest list, selecting only those family members and friends who are truly an important part of your lives. If you find yourselves saying things like, "But if we invite Aunt Susan, we have to invite cousin Tony," than an intimate wedding may not work for you. However, if you're both content to have a small number of guests, then start planning!

Just because your wedding will be small doesn't mean it won't be very special and original. You can marry at the foot of the Eiffel Tower in Paris, say your vows in a city synagogue, or opt for a garden ceremony and afternoon tea party.

# ASK THE EXPERTS

**My fiancé and I want to have a very intimate wedding with only our parents, siblings, and a few friends. My brother is casually dating a girl he recently met. Is it rude to tell him that she isn't invited?**

Gently explain to your brother why you have chosen to have an intimate wedding. Let him know that you would appreciate it if he didn't bring his new girlfriend to the wedding. Make sure you are consistent with other single invitees. You've made a decision to take your vows in front of the special people in your life. Do what makes you feel comfortable.

**Our guest list consists of 10 people, but most reception facilities are geared toward larger groups. What to do?**

Contact nontraditional locations such as art museums or galleries, which often feature private rooms for small gatherings. Inquire whether your favorite restaurant can accommodate a private party. Or try contacting a botanical garden or a few bed-and-breakfasts.

**We're hosting an intimate wedding with a guest list of 20. Every baker we've contacted has told us that we have to purchase a wedding cake that serves a minimum of 50!**

Here's a tip: Don't tell him it's for a wedding. Simply state that you are having a party and would like a white cake for 20 people. Or ask your baker to create 20 miniature, single-serving cakes. These are all the rage at high-society weddings, and you can use this trend to your advantage!

# destination weddings

**Far and away vows**

A getaway wedding—or **destination** wedding—is one that takes place in a location other than the bride's, or groom's home-town. It's an increasingly popular choice for those who have friends and family scattered all over the country (and who also can afford to travel). Popular getaway wedding spots are usually resorts located in Florida, Hawaii, and Las Vegas. Other resort locations that are especially conducive to getaway weddings are Puerto Rico, the U.S. Virgin Islands, the Bahamas, Bermuda, and Jamaica.

Just remember, you are asking guests to make a significant invest-ment in time and money to attend your celebration. Realize that some people—even those very dear to you—may not be able to attend. So before you make any decisions, ask around to make sure that those you want to come can make it. Etiquette demands that wedding invitations to destination weddings be mailed out at least 10 weeks in advance of the wedding date. (For more on invitations, see page 116.)

Planning for a destination wedding takes a bit more organization. It's a good idea to hire a professional wedding planner (see page 72) with a successful track record of creating magical events at the location of your choice.

## STEP BY STEP
### Getaway Wedding Checklist

1. Set your budget.

2. Settle on a guest count.

3. Research your options by calling resorts, tourism departments, travel agencies, and destination wedding planners.

4. Ask for references, and check them!

5. Apply for a passport, if necessary, at least six months before the wedding.

6. Check seasonal weather, and avoid traditionally "off" months.

7. Get the details in writing, and book your event. Use credit cards for deposits.

8. Double-check arrangements a month before the wedding, and make sure marriage-license requirements are met.

9. If necessary, rent a tuxedo for your fiancé, and bring it with you.

10. Leave a spare house key with a friend who isn't attending, so if you forget to pack something important, it can be shipped to you.

## INTERVIEW THE EXPERT / Destination Planner

### Norma Kennedy
### Director of Weddings at Marriott's Beach Resort on St. Thomas

■ Never plan your wedding on a travel day, unless you're arriving by cruise ship. You don't want bags under your eyes for your special photos!

■ Always carry your wedding gown on the plane, and take all other wedding necessities in carry-on bags (in case your luggage doesn't make it to the wedding).

■ Most importantly, be relaxed on your special day! Let your wedding coordinator worry about the cake being perfect, the champagne being chilled, and the gazebo being decorated, not to mention the officiant, photographer, musicians, and flowers.

# exotic destination weddings

**Going for the far-flung**

*I*f a destination wedding intrigues you—and your families can afford it—why not let your imagination go wild? Always wanted to be married under the stars in Fiji or on a gondola in Venice? Go for it! Once you've chosen your location, hire a wedding planner who specializes in destination weddings. Aside from helping you secure a group travel rate, he or she will know the area, available local services, and customs. Consider contacting A Wedding for You, wedding planners who have done it all, including events in the Caribbean, Alaska, Australia, Prague, Venice, Scotland, Switzerland, Mexico, Hawaii, California, Florida and New York City. Contact them at 800-929-4198 or log on to **www.awedding-foryou.com**.

Wedding specialist Beverly Clark offers a getaway wedding-location clearinghouse at **www.weddinglocation.com**. Search for resorts and wedding coordinators in the areas you're considering, and request more information via e-mail.

## Budget Saver

**M**any Caribbean resorts offer "free" weddings to couples who plan to honeymoon several nights at their hotel. Contact these resorts for more information:

Sandals, **www.sandals.com**, 888-SANDALS
Swept Away, **www.sweptaway.com**, 800-545-7937
Beaches, **www.beaches.com**, 888-BEACHES
SuperClubs, **www.superclubs.com**, 800-GO-SUPER

## Can't-Be-Beat Getaway Wedding Destinations

**Orlando**

Disney's Fairy Tale Weddings department helps thousands of couples each year. Their economical Intimate Wedding includes a ceremony, along with a cake/champagne reception and a four-night honeymoon stay at a deluxe resort. The sky's the limit with their Custom Wedding, which can take place throughout Walt Disney World—including inside the theme parks. Intimate Weddings start at $3,333, and Custom Weddings begin at $7,500. Celebrations at Cinderella Castle start at $35,000.

Call Walt Disney World in Orlando, Florida, at 407-828-3400; Disneyland in Anaheim, California, at 714-956-6527; or log on to **www.disneyweddings.com**.

If an Orlando wedding is for you but Disney isn't, call the following officiants, who can arrange beautiful ceremonies throughout central Florida: Reverend Tim Herring of Central Florida Weddings and Vow Renewals (**http://home.att.net/~revtim/**, 407-876-6433) or Reverend Jack Day (**www.revjackday.com**, 407-579-8711).

**St. Thomas**

Weddings in Paradise at the Marriott Beach Resorts (Frenchman's Reef and Morning Star) on St. Thomas offers four terrific packages, starting at only $550. For your ceremony, select a gazebo perched on a bluff overlooking the sea, or wait until sunset and enjoy your nuptials while sailing the Caribbean (**www.offshoreresorts.com/stthomas**, 800-FOR-LOVE. All other Marriott resorts also provide wedding packages—visit **www.marriott.com**).

# make your themes
# come true

**Fairy tales
for sale**

*A* terrific way to add spice to your celebration is to host a **theme wedding**. A theme can be as simple as incorporating a single element—such as stars—throughout your big day. Consider star-studded invitations and ceremony programs, star confetti on reception tables and a star-accented wedding cake. Just pick an idea or subject you adore and run with it! Some possibilities include: angels, celestial motifs, roses, Christmas, doves, hearts, ivy, oceans, beaches, or even a military theme.

Another alternative is to use history as your guide and to produce a Victorian, medieval or Renaissance wedding. To dress the part, check out vintage wedding gowns and attire at **www.vintagewedding.com** (800-660-3640). If you want your guests to be in on the dress-up fun, costumes can be purchased at The Renaissance Store (**www.renstore.com**, 800-730-KING). Many Renaissance festivals—such as the Texas Scarborough Faire (**www.scarboroughrenfest.com**)—offer wedding packages that include costume rentals for you and your guests, a town crier, and a reception menu of turkey legs and grilled quail. Pick up the *Medieval Wedding Guide* by Vanessa Hand for everything you need to know to plan this type of event (also available as an e-book at **www.owl-lady.com**).

If you have a hankering for a western wedding, you'll want to pay a visit to Renton Western Wear (**www.cowboycountrywedding.com**, 888-273-7039). They offer custom-made Old West gowns, bridal boots and hats, grooms' attire, and other accessories.

## When You Wish Upon a Star

In a small bridal boutique in Celebration, Florida, many brides have found their fairy godmother in Shelley Geery and her shop, Impressions (**www.fairytalewedding.com**, 407-566-8072). Over the years, Shelley has custom-designed wedding invitations, ceremony programs, favors, and other decor accents for couples re-creating Cinderella's Ball, "Beauty and the Beast"–inspired events, and those where the guests of honor are two mice: Mickey and Minnie. Impressions is also the only place where you can order the signature white-chocolate cake topper that Walt Disney World uses for its spectacular wedding cakes.

Looking for more pixie dust to sprinkle on your wedding celebration? Call Disney at 407-824-2856. They sell exclusive Disney-theme wedding accessories that you won't find anywhere else.

If you're dreaming of a Victorian motif, tie the knot at the Precious Moments Victorian Wedding Island in Carthage, Missouri (**www.pmweddings.com**, 800-543-7975 ext. 3028). Samuel J. Butcher—artist and originator of the Precious Moments collection of figurines—has created a full-service wedding "island." You'll find an old-fashioned chapel on the water, a Victorian bridal house for all the day's preparations, and a Victorian Mansion circa 1885 for the reception.

# elopements

**Just the two of us
(maybe)**

*W*hile **elopements** are by far the fastest way to marry, you both still have to apply (usually in advance) for your marriage license and comply with the waiting period (anywhere from 10 minutes to five days, depending on the state in which you are getting married). What happens when you elope? You and your beloved will go to a courthouse or other official office and see a justice of the peace, who will ask you to say your vows (typically traditional ones), have you sign the wedding certificate and will pronounce you married. Two witnesses are also required to sign the certificate. You can ask two friends along, or the official can provide them. It all usually takes about 15 minutes.

Just because an elopement is an instant wedding, it doesn't mean it can't be special. Bring a camera or hire a wedding photojournalist to take a few pictures. Most justices will let you read a special poem or say your own vows. Closure is vital to all ceremonies, elopements included. Have a bottle of champagne on hand to celebrate with afterward or go for a special meal at a favorite restaurant.

## Let's Just Elope

*I*f you're thinking about running off and getting married, pick up a copy of Scott Shaw and Lynn Beahan's *Let's Elope: The Definitive Guide to Eloping, Destination Weddings and Other Creative Options*. Included is a quiz that will help you figure out whether eloping is right for you. Questions to ponder include:

Can you keep a secret?
Are you impulsive?
Do you care what your parents think about your wedding plans?
Do you love adventure?
What is your budget?

# ASK THE EXPERTS

**We've heard that Las Vegas is a great place to elope. Is that true?**

You heard right! Las Vegas ranks as the number-one eloping location in the United States, in part because Nevada has no waiting period and a large number of its wedding chapels and resort casinos are open 24 hours a day. Here are some favorites:

- Bally's Celebration Wedding Chapel,
  **www.ballyschapel.com**, 800-872-1211

- Wedding Chapels at Bellagio,
  **www.bellagiolasvegas.com**, 888-987-3344

- Caesars Palace Wedding Chapel,
  **www.caesars.com**, 877-279-3334

- The Elvis Chapel,
  **www.elvischapel.com**, 800-452-6081

- Little Chapel of the Flowers,
  **www.littlechapel.com**, 800-843-2410

- Wedding Chapels at Mandalay Bay,
  **www.mandalaybay.com**, 877-632-7701

- MGM Forever Grand Chapel,
  **www.mgmgrand.com**, 800-646-5530

- Monte Carlo Wedding Chapel,
  **www.monte-carlo.com**, 800-822-8651

- Paris Chapel,
  **www.parislasvegas.com**, 877-650-5021

- Weddings at The Venetian,
  **www.venetian.com**, 877-883-6423

## An Affair to Remember

Each Valentine's Day, 14 lucky couples are married on the 80th floor Sky Lobby of the Empire State Building. The ceremony is free, but you have to win a contest first. Write a letter explaining how you met your intended and why you'd like to marry at the Empire State Building (including photographs or poems with your letter can increase your chances). Winners get a ceremony only, so you'll have to dream up the rest of your wedding day. The contest deadline is December 31 for the following February. Send entries to: The Empire State Building Observatory, 350 Fifth Avenue, Suite 8004, New York, New York 10118.

# second time around

**Rewriting the etiquette of second marriages**

*M*arrying for a second—or third—time is a special wedding experience. You've got the wisdom of a previous marriage behind you and the promise of a new beginning in front of you. Feel free to have the wedding of your dreams, especially since you can forego the mistakes from your past wedding ceremonies. Don't let anyone tell you that you can't wear white, have a large wedding, or invite your ex-spouse to the festivities if you're still on good terms. The great thing about a second or third marriage is that the rules are being rewritten by encore brides every day.

Of course, there are a few things you'll have to do differently. If you have children, for instance, they should be told before anyone else; then inform your parents. And chances are you will want to include your children in your new marriage ceremony. First marriages are usually announced by the bride's parents. This time, announce the good tidings yourselves, or let your older children put an announcement in the local newspaper for you.

The rest of your plans can proceed once you determine your budget (you'll most likely be paying for this wedding yourselves), wedding style, and ceremony preferences. If one or both of you is religious, you'll have to address any stipulations your religions put on second marriages.

#  Ask the Experts

**We both have children from previous marriages. How can we make them important participants in our wedding day?**

■ Have your son walk you down the aisle or serve as best man or an usher.

■ Ask your daughter to be your maid of honor, bridesmaid, or flower girl.

■ Ask older children to do a reading at the ceremony.

■ Incorporate a family medallion (**www.familymedallion.com**) presentation into your ceremony. This tradition utilizes a piece of jewelry (either a pin or a necklace with a medallion) with three circles of intertwined silver or gold, symbolizing wife, husband, children. After you and your fiancé exchange your vows, you make additional promises to your children and present them with the family medallion ring or a pin symbolizing the union of your families.

■ Write vows to your children and read them at the ceremony after you read your marriage vows.

■ Hold your wedding at a child-friendly location, and scrap the traditional honeymoon for a family vacation instead. This is a wonderful opportunity to bond with the new members of your immediate family.

**I know that thousands of couples are marrying for the second time, but it's tough to find information about it in magazines and books. Any suggestions?**

*Bride Again* is a great magazine dedicated to helping encore brides plan the perfect event. This quarterly magazine can be purchased on newsstands or at bookstores nationwide (**www.brideagain.com**, 714-632-7000 for subscription information). Several good books are also listed in the resource section at the end of this chapter.

# now what do I do?
## Answers to common questions

**What if we determine our wedding style but can't make it happen?**

Often a couple dreams about a fantasy wedding, such as marrying on a Hawaiian beach, only to come crashing back to reality when their budget can't handle it. Planning a wedding is often a compromise. If you can't go to Hawaii, for instance, have Hawaii come to you: Ask your baker to create a passion-fruit wedding cake, and decorate reception tables with seashells, wear an orchid lei instead of carrying a bouquet, and serve a luau-inspired meal.

**We'd like to marry on the bridge of the U.S.S. Enterprise at Star Trek: The Experience in the Las Vegas Hilton. Our guests will dress up as Klingons and other series characters. Is this a crazy idea?**

Crazy? No. Unusual? Most definitely! You and your fiancé are obviously fans of the genre. If this will make your wedding dreams come true—and if your guests are willing to play along—go for it! For more information about weddings "aboard" the U.S.S. Enterprise, call 702-697-8750 or visit **www.startrekexp.com**.

**I love the idea of a theme wedding. Since we're marrying during the Christmas season, we've chosen a holly and ivy theme. Any ideas?**

If your wedding is more than a year away, watch for after-Christmas sales where you can pick up decor accents. After Valentine's Day is another great time to buy discounted items, such as white and red candles. Start by selecting an invitation with a holly and ivy design. Ask your florist to create a bouquet of red and white roses, plus sprigs of holly and ivy. Create pew bows accented with your motif for the ceremony. Carry this theme through to the reception, where your table centerpieces can be a re-creation of your bouquet. For favors, why not give small pots of ivy? Decorate the pots with your names and wedding date. (Grow ivy clippings several months before your wedding and replant them in smaller clay pots, or get them at your local garden center.)

**This is my second marriage. I really want a big wedding so that I can share my joy with friends and family. Does this go against tradition?**

In the past, second marriages were downplayed, but that attitude is changing. If you want to wear a white gown and have a full-scale reception in a hall, do it! You've been blessed to find your soul mate, and there is no reason to be quiet about it. Celebrate however you want!

# NOW WHERE DO I GO?!

## THEME WEDDINGS WEB SITES

A Vintage Wedding
**www.vintagewedding.com**, 800-660-3640

Renton Western Wear
**www.cowboycountrywedding.com**,
888-273-7039

Franck's Bridal Studio at
Disney's Wedding Pavilion
407-824-3094

Impressions
**www.fairytalewedding.com**, 407-566-8072

Chivalry Sports Renaissance Store
**www.renstore.com**, 800-730-KING

## DESTINATION WEDDINGS WEB SITES

A Wedding For You
**www.aweddingforyou.com**, 800-929-4198

Beverly Clark's Wedding Location
**www.weddinglocation.com**, 800-933-3434

Disney's Fairy Tale Weddings
**www.disneyweddings.com**, Orlando,
Florida: 407-828-3400; Anaheim,
California: 714-956-6527

Getaway Weddings
**www.getawayweddings.com**

## BOOKS

**For the Bride: A Guide to
Style and Gracious Living**
by Colin Cowie

**Real Wedding: A Celebration
of Personal Style**
by Sally Kilbridge

**Let's Elope: The Definitive Guide to
Eloping, Destination Weddings and
Other Creative Options**
by Scott Shaw and Lynn Beahan

**Beyond Vegas: 25 Exotic Wedding
and Elopement Destinations Around
the World**
by Lisa Tabb and Sam Silverstein

**Storybook Weddings: A Guide to Fun
and Romantic Theme Weddings**
by Robin A. Kring

**Wedding Plans: 50 Unique Themes for
the Wedding of Your Dreams**
by Sharon Dlugosch

**Weddings, a Family Affair: The New
Etiquette for Second Marriages and
Couples With Divorced Parents**
by Marjorie Engle and Beverly Clark

**1,001 Ways to Have a Dazzling
Second Wedding**
by Sharon Naylor

You can host the perfect wedding and stay within your budget. Don't worry if you have caviar tastes and a tuna fish budget! With the proper planning, you can have the celebration of a lifetime without going broke.

# Wedding Costs

# setting the date

## Selecting the ideal time and place

$\mathscr{I}$t's time to set the date. Believe it or not, your selection will partially determine how much you'll pay for various wedding services, not to mention how many of the people from your guest list will attend. This is because, as with many other industries, there is a high (popular) and a low (off-peak) season for wedding celebrations. Traditionally, May through October are prime months for weddings (although certain holidays, such as Valentine's Day and New Year's Eve, also cause a spike on the wedding-o-meter). If you wish to take advantage of off-peak discounts, consider getting married between November and April.

However, if you live in an area of the country that gets rough winter weather, there are plenty of reasons to steer clear of a white wedding. Your best bet may be to plan your wedding during the **shoulder season**—between the peak and off-peak dates. For example, an April wedding in Boston may be ideal.

You will be competing with corporate holiday parties if you schedule a Christmas-time wedding.

Consider the pros and cons of scheduling your event on a holiday weekend. While it may be convenient for you, there could be downsides for your guests. Air travel usually costs more during a holiday since most are considered **blackout dates**, which means discounts and frequent-flier miles can't be used. In addition, your guests may have family vacations scheduled around certain long weekends.

And if you wish to schedule a Christmastime event, remember that you'll be vying for reception space with corporate holiday parties, year-end banquets, and the like.

# The Pros and Cons of Each Month

**JANUARY** Pros: Off-peak
Cons: Cold weather and snow can be a problem in some locations; avoid New Year's Day; rainy season in the South

**FEBRUARY** Pros: Off-peak
Cons: Cold weather and snow can be a problem in some locations; avoid Valentine's Day; rainy season in the South

**MARCH** Pros: Off-peak
Cons: Cold weather and snow can be a problem in some locations; rainy season in the South

**APRIL** Pros: Off-peak; pleasant weather
Cons: Can still get chilly (avoid sleeveless gowns)

**MAY** Pros: Gorgeous weather
Cons: Peak

**JUNE** Pros: Gorgeous weather
Cons: Peak; threat of afternoon thunderstorms in some areas

**JULY** Pros: Gorgeous weather
Cons: Peak; heat; threat of afternoon thunderstorms in some areas

**AUGUST** Pros: Gorgeous weather
Cons: Peak; humidity; heat; threat of afternoon thunderstorms in some areas

**SEPTEMBER** Pros: Pleasant weather
Cons: Peak; hurricane season; threat of afternoon thunderstorms in some areas

**OCTOBER** Pros: Pleasant weather but can get chilly (avoid sleeveless gowns)
Cons: Peak; hurricane season

**NOVEMBER** Pros: Off-peak
Cons: Holiday rush; hurricane season

**DECEMBER** Pros: Off-peak
Cons: Holiday rush; avoid Christmas Day/Eve and New Year's Eve

# who pays for what

**Money changes
everything**

*Y*ou and your intended—and your families—may have an
argument or two about your wedding, and it will most likely be
about money. Emotions run high during wedding planning, and
adding financial concerns to the mix can be downright explosive!
Protect yourselves from the very beginning by determining who
will pay for what. Don't stop there, though. Draw up a clear **budget** for each item so that there are no surprises later (see page 66
for more information).

Traditionally, the bride's family foots the bill for most wedding
expenses, including the wedding gown, invitations, officiant, limousine transportation, reception-site fees, music, food and beverages, decorations, favors, photography, and videography.

The groom's family generally pays for flowers and
the rehearsal dinner. The groom pays for the engagement ring and the wedding **bands** (rings). And he or
his parents pick up the tab for the honeymoon.

Tradition, however, is not all it's cracked up to be! Today, wedding
expenses can be broken down in any manner your families see fit.
The "average" wedding, with 175 guests, costs $18,000. If your parents are not in a position to pay for your entire wedding, consider
taking on this responsibility yourselves. Often the groom's family
may also offer financial help. Find out what's best for your family,
and create a budget that works for everyone involved.

If you've been married before, don't expect your parents to pay
for too much unless they are financially able (and then only if
they want to).

## ASK THE EXPERTS

**We want to pay for our own wedding, partly so we'll have total control over all decisions. When we told my parents, they got very upset because they feel it's their obligation to pay for the wedding.**

It's kind of your parents to want to finance your wedding. However, it also sounds like you feel there may be some strings attached. Tell Mom and Dad how you envision your wedding, and ask if their offer to pay for your event includes this vision. If they paint a different picture, let them know how much you appreciate their offer but that you have your heart set on something else. They may still want to give you their financial support, but be clear that if you accept their money, you'll listen to their suggestions but you won't necessarily act on them.

**My fiancé's family is Italian, and they've offered to pay for a dessert table and beautifully wrappped candy-covered almonds as favors for our reception. My parents, who are paying for everything else, are complaining that the wedding is being "taken over by the other side."**

The goal of wedding planning is to create a special day reflecting the love that you share as a couple. Explain to your parents that this is a family tradition that your fiancé's family wants to share with them. That's why they've been generous enough to offer to pay for it. Have your fiancé speak with your parents as well. This is not a case of one-upmanship—it's about combining the traditions and customs of two families.

# pampered guests

**Keeping friends and family informed**

*Y*our wedding is all about you and your fiancé. However, it's also about gathering the people you love so that they can celebrate with you. As such, it's very important that you're a good hostess. Depending on the type of wedding you've chosen, your friends and family will need to be informed. You have several options: have your bridesmaids handle spreading the latest information or send out **save-the-date cards** and/or **newsletters**. These are to be followed by formal invitations. See pages 116-117.

Save-the-date cards are sent by couples planning a destination wedding. While not an official invitation, save-the-date notices are sent prior to the invitation to everyone on the guest list to let them know the date and location of the wedding. This way, guests can start securing necessary vacation time from work, purchasing airline tickets, and reserving hotel rooms.

Newsletters are another option. They're generally sent to guests after the invitations have gone out but before the actual wedding. The contents are up to the individual couple but can include the story of how you met, detailed information about the reception site, directions to the ceremony, and more. It's also a great way to share information about hotels and car-rental agencies.

In addition, if you have a large number of family members flying in from another city, consider arranging a **group discount** with an airline and a hotel. Most major carriers offer discount programs to guests traveling to and from weddings. Contact these airlines for further information: Delta Meeting Network (**www.delta.com**, 800-241-6108), America Airlines Wedding Event Travel (**www.aa.com**, 800-221-2255), Continental MeetingWorks (**www.continental.com**, 800-468-7022), US Airways Weddings (**www.usair.com**, 877-874-7687) and United Airlines Meetings and Conventions (**www.unitedairlines.com**, 800-MEET-UAL). Most hotels will also let you reserve a block of rooms at a discount.

## ASK THE EXPERTS

**We've arranged a room block at a local hotel for our out-of-town guests, but so far only two couples have booked rooms! The hotel wants to know how long they should hold the rooms. What should I do?**

If you have reserved rooms for your guests, it's a good idea to tell them about it on the invitation. Simply state that rooms at a discount price will be held until a certain date. Phone or e-mail your out-of-town guests and ask them where they'll be staying (and gently remind them that if they want to stay in the hotel you chose, they'll need to book a room soon).

**We're planning our wedding, and there's a three-hour gap between our ceremony and the reception. I don't think it's a big deal, but my fiancé says it's rude to our guests. Why?**

No doubt you and your groom will find something to keep you occupied for three hours—taking photos, for instance. It would be a drag for your guests, though, if they had to return home or to a hotel room for several hours. So that you don't break the momentum of your special day, it's best to schedule your wedding-day events closer together.

## FIRST PERSON DISASTER STORY

### Unhappy Guests

We got married in an old New England town that's home to a famous hotel. I blocked a set of rooms at a discount for our wedding guests, but forgot to mention that in our wedding newsletter. At the wedding, my bridesmaid told me that some guests were grumbling about the hotel prices. I contacted the hotel, but they said unless the guests stated that they were with our wedding party, they couldn't get the discounted rate. It had been my responsibility to tell them I had reserved the rooms for them, not the hotel's.

**Mary B., Kennebunkport, Maine**

# wedding time line

**All in good time**

*W*hile some tasks can be handled in a short amount of time, some things—like gown shopping or writing your vows—usually take a lot more time than you originally anticipated. That's why it's good to overestimate the amount of time you'll need to carry out certain tasks. Below, you'll find a traditional wedding-planning schedule. Each couple is different, so take a look at these suggestions and tweak your schedule accordingly.

| 12 MONTHS BEFORE THE WEDDING | 11 TO 9 MONTHS PRIOR | 8 TO 6 MONTHS PRIOR | 2 TO 5 MONTHS PRIOR |
|---|---|---|---|
| ▪ Announce your engagement.<br><br>▪ Buy a datebook with lots of room for appointments and notes.<br><br>▪ Determine your wedding style.<br><br>▪ Sit down with your fiancé and your parents to create a budget.<br><br>▪ Decide who will pay for what.<br><br>▪ Set your wedding date.<br><br>▪ Ask your families to draw up their guest-list requests, and estimate a rough guest count.<br><br>▪ Begin gown shopping.<br><br>▪ Select your wedding party.<br><br>▪ Research, select, and reserve your ceremony and reception sites.<br><br>▪ Determine if you will use a wedding consultant (see page 72); interview and hire someone you feel comfortable with. | ▪ Book your caterer, photographer, videographer, baker, musicians, and florist.<br><br>▪ Select your officiant (see page 79) and meet with him or her to determine the style of your ceremony.<br><br>▪ Register for gifts.<br><br>▪ Order your wedding gown and bridal accessories.<br><br>▪ Choose and order dresses for your bridesmaids.<br><br>▪ Start researching honeymoon options (see pages 171-195). | ▪ Select and order invitations and thank-you cards.<br><br>▪ Plan special touches with all wedding vendors.<br><br>▪ Reserve hotel room block for out-of-town guests.<br><br>▪ Arrange discount travel options with airlines and car-rental agencies. | ▪ Select tuxedos for ushers.<br><br>▪ Select cake style.<br><br>▪ Choose a reception menu and beverages.<br><br>▪ Finalize the guest list.<br><br>▪ Inquire about marriage-license requirements at the county clerk's office.<br><br>▪ Get a blood test, if necessary.<br><br>▪ Make honeymoon reservations.<br><br>▪ Secure any necessary travel documents, such as passports.<br><br>▪ Choose and order your wedding bands. |

| 4 TO 10 WEEKS PRIOR | 2 TO 3 WEEKS PRIOR | 1 WEEK PRIOR | THE DAY BEFORE THE WEDDING |
|---|---|---|---|
| ■ Mail invitations six to eight weeks before the wedding. | ■ Create a seating chart. | ■ Pack for your honeymoon. | ■ Relax! |
| ■ Pick music for the reception. At the very least, write a "Do Not Play This Song!" list for the D.J. | ■ Confirm all details with your vendors. | | ■ Spend some time with family and friends. |
| | ■ Give your caterer the final guest count. | | ■ Attend rehearsal and rehearsal dinner. |
| ■ Purchase thank-you gifts for the wedding party. | ■ Send request lists to the photographer, videographer, and musicians. | | ■ Get some sleep! |
| ■ Do a hair and makeup trial run. | ■ Get your marriage license. | ■ Determine gratuities for each vendor and place amount in envelopes to be given out at the wedding. | |
| ■ Get your gown fitted. | ■ Confirm honeymoon reservations. | ■ Confirm final guest count with the caterer. | |

65

# money matters

## Slicing the wedding budget pie

*O*nce you've established your budget, it's time to allocate those resources to the various pieces of the wedding-day puzzle. Most couples choose to divvy up their budget among the following categories (Note: Prices vary from region to region):

| Category | % of Budget | $10,000 Budget | $20,000 Budget | $30,000 Budget |
|---|---|---|---|---|
| **Food & Beverages** | 30% | $3,000 | $6,000 | $9,000 |
| **Attire** | 10% | $1,000 | $2,000 | $3,000 |
| **Site Fees** | 10% | $1,000 | $2,000 | $3,000 |
| **Photography & Videography** | 10% | $1,000 | $2,000 | $3,000 |
| **Flowers & Decor** | 10% | $1,000 | $2,000 | $3,000 |
| **Music & Entertainment** | 10% | $1,000 | $2,000 | $3,000 |
| **Transportation** | 8% | $ 800 | $1,600 | $2,400 |
| **Miscellaneous** | 5% | $ 500 | $1,000 | $1,500 |
| **Gifts & Favors** | 5% | $ 500 | $1,000 | $1,500 |
| **Stationery** | 2% | $ 200 | $ 400 | $ 600 |

Depending on your budget, you may be able to tweak individual categories to maximize the money you have to spend. For example, if you have a $30,000 budget but you choose not to hire limousine transportation, you can save 8 percent right off the top of your budget. That money can go toward another category that you'd prefer to focus on.

# ASK THE EXPERTS

**Is it true that the average wedding with 175 guests costs about $20,000?**

Yes, it's true. But remember that where you live has a lot to do with how much you'll pay, since items will cost more in metropolitan or resort areas. That said, weddings are expensive, which is why you should really research and plan to have the wedding you really want.

**We're on a tight budget. Any ideas on how to host a wedding reception with $7,500?**

You can host a nice, low-key affair on a budget. Consider marrying at your home or church hall to avoid extravagant site fees. Purchase a discontinued wedding gown off the rack. Ask a friend to bake your wedding cake. Buy flowers in bulk two days before your wedding, and have your bridesmaids help you create the bouquets, boutonnieres, and centerpieces. How much money you spend on your wedding day isn't the point—it's how much love you put into the event.

**My fiancé and I are both musicians, so music will be an important part of our wedding. Can we spend a large portion of our budget on entertainment?**

Of course! Take a look at everything in your budget. Select one or two categories that aren't that important to you (for example, stationery and videography), and minimize your expenditures in those areas. Then use the money you save to bankroll top-of-the-line entertainment. Or ask your musician friends to play in lieu of a gift.

## Taxes and Gratuities

For vendor fees, don't forget to factor in state sales tax and a gratuity (which generally ranges from 16 to 20 percent). These fees have a huge impact on big-ticket items such as food and beverages. Make sure to include these charges when tallying your expenditures.

# three budget scenarios

## $15,000 BUDGET FOR 150 GUESTS

- **Wedding Attire**
  Gown and accessories, $500
  Tuxedo, $100
  Wedding rings, $400
- **Invitations**
  Selected from mail-order catalog, $300
- **Legal Fees**
  Marriage license, $30
  Officiant, $200
- **Transportation**
  Two eight-passenger limousines
      (home to church, church to
      reception hall), $750
  Luxury sedan (point-to-point
      transportation for bride and groom
      after the reception), $50
- **Site Fee**
  Banquet hall with outdoor gazebo (cere-
  mony fee), $500
- **Photography and Videography**
  Photographer, $1,000
  No videographer
- **Flowers**
  Carnations and calla lilies, $2,300
- **Music and Entertainment**
  Organist at ceremony, $200
  D.J. at reception, $1,000
- **Lunchtime Reception**
  Plated meal (salad, chicken, potato,
  vegetable, and wedding cake, plus 6 percent
  meal tax and 20 percent gratuity),
  $35 per person, for a total of $6,600

- **Cash Bar**
  Bartender fee, $500
- **Gifts and Favors**
  Costume jewelry for three bridesmaids, $100
  Watches for three ushers, $100
  Votive-candle favors for guests, $300

## $30,000 BUDGET FOR 150 GUESTS

- **Wedding Attire**
  Gown and accessories, $1,000
  Tuxedo, $200
  Wedding rings, $1,000
- **Invitations**
  Selected at a stationer, $500
- **Legal Fees**
  Marriage license, $30
  Officiant, $270
- **Transportation**
  Two 10-passenger limousines (home to
      church, church to reception hall),
      $1,100
  Rolls Royce getaway car (for bride and
      groom after the reception), $500
- **Site Fee**
  Church ceremony, $300
  Art gallery reception, $1,500
- **Photography and Videography**
  Photographer, $2,500
  Videographer, $1,000
- **Flowers**
  Lilies of the valley and roses, $3,700
- **Music and Entertainment**
  String quartet at ceremony, $595
  D.J. at reception, $1,500

- **Evening Reception**

  Passed hors d'oeuvres, buffet dinner stations (pasta station, prime-rib carving station, seafood-crepe station, and wedding cake, plus 6 percent meal tax and 20 percent gratuity), $50 per person, for a total of $9,450

- **Hosted Bar**

  Call brands for three hours, (plus 6 percent meal tax and 20 percent gratuity), $20 per person, for a total of $3,800

- **Gifts and Favors**

  Snow globes for five bridesmaids, $300

  Watches for five ushers, $300

  Godiva chocolate-truffle favors for guests, $400

# $45,000 BUDGET FOR 150 GUESTS

- **Wedding Attire**

  Gown and accessories, $2,000

  Tuxedo, $400

  Wedding rings, $2,000

- **Invitations**

  Custom-designed, handmade invitations, $1,000

- **Legal Fees**

  Marriage license, $30

  Officiant, $270

- **Transportation**

  Horse-drawn carriage for bride, $1,200

  Two 10-passenger limousines (home to church, church to reception hall), $1,100

  Rolls Royce getaway car (for bride and groom after the reception), $500

- **Site Fee**

  Cathedral ceremony, $800

  Reception on a private yacht, $2,000

- **Photography and Videography**

  Photographer, $3,000

  Videographer, $1,500

- **Flowers**

  Roses, $3,400

- **Music and Entertainment**

  Organist at ceremony, $300

  Professional vocalist at ceremony, $300

  Jazz trio at reception, $2,000

- **Evening Reception**

  Seafood extravaganza with a make-your-own ice cream sundae dessert bar and wedding cake (plus 6 percent meal tax and 20 percent gratuity), $75 per person, for a total of $14,200

- **Hosted Bar**

  Premium brands for three hours (plus 6 percent meal tax and 20 percent gratuity), $30 per person, for a total of $5,700

  Champagne toast, $1,200

- **Gifts and Favors**

  Snow globes for five bridesmaids, $300

  Watches for five ushers, $300

  A red rose for each female guest and a cigar for each male guest, $500

# paying for it

## Dos and don'ts

*P*aying for a wedding is quite an undertaking. If you are still unclear about who will be paying for what, sit down with your fiancé and your families and decide right now. This will prevent a lot of confusion in the future.

Whoever is paying the bills will be writing a lot of checks. This is because, most often, wedding-service providers request a deposit in order to secure the date. Whenever possible, you should use your credit card for these deposits because this provides you with added purchase protection. If something goes wrong (say, the florist never shows up), you simply contact your credit card company and they'll have your deposit refunded.

As long as you're spending this money, use the expenditures to your advantage. Charging purchases on your credit cards—and paying them off—will help you build your credit. And if you have a card that offers rewards for each dollar spent, take advantage of it! Many couples earn enough frequent-flier miles to convert into free airline tickets for a second honeymoon.

If the wedding or honeymoon of your dreams is out of reach because of a lack of funds, do not apply for a loan. Beginning your marriage under a pile of debt is never a good idea, since it will surely become a source of tension in the future. Your best bet is to wait until you've saved enough for the wedding that you want.

# ASK THE EXPERTS

**We've got two months to go before our wedding, and I've decided that I want to use a different photographer than the one we originally contracted with a few months ago. I requested a refund on our deposit, but the photographer says it's nonrefundable. Is there anything I can do?**

No, not really. When you decide on the vendors for your wedding celebration, choose carefully. Once you sign a contract and put down a deposit, you are committed. It's your prerogative to change your mind down the road, but you'll forfeit your deposit and you may even owe the vendor a cancellation fee. Remember, these vendors are in business, and if you book a date and then back out, that vendor has just lost a sale. Double-check all your contracts before signing them, and be sure that these are the professionals you want to work with.

**Some credit card companies offer cash back on a percentage of the amount charged each year. Is it worth getting one of these cards and using it for all wedding-related purchases?**

Yes, but choose the credit card carefully. What is the annual fee? What is the interest rate? What is the fee for late payments? Because of the cash-back option, your interest fee may be higher, so be sure to pay off as much of the debt as you can each month.

**How much does the average honeymoon cost?**

According to *Bride's* magazine's Millennium Report on honeymoon travel, the average honeymoon costs $3,500.

## Wedding Insurance

Do you always worry about everything? Then you may wish to purchase insurance for your wedding. Policies generally cover cancellation or postponement of the event, as well as loss coverage for photography and videography, wedding attire, gifts, rings, and deposits. Call your insurance agent for details, or contact WedSafe (**www.wedsafe.com**, 877-SAFE-WED) or Fireman's Fund (**www.firemansfund.com**, 800-227-1700).

# hiring a wedding planner

## The right consultant for you

$\mathscr{H}$iring a **wedding planner** (someone who coordinates all aspects of your wedding for a fee) may be just the thing to save you from being overwhelmed by all the research and planning. A planner can help you with the style and scope of your wedding, your budget, etiquette, and the creation of a personalized wedding calendar.

Another plus: Each day, planners coordinate weddings in your area. That means they know the best sites in town and the best wedding service providers in the area. And because they're always booking events, they can wield more power at the bargaining table when trying to negotiate prices. This alone can be worth their fee.

Pricing and services vary from coordinator to coordinator, but all offer three levels of service:

■ Full-service coordination: Help with everything from establishing the budget to mailing wedding invitations to overseeing the ceremony. Average cost: $2,000 to $3,000. Some full-service planners prefer to base their fee on the wedding budget. They charge 10 percent to 15 percent of the entire wedding bill.

■ Partial coordination: Help hiring and overseeing vendors, plus organizing the ceremony. Average cost: $1,000 to $1,500.

■ Rehearsal and ceremony only: Help organizing and overseeing the rehearsal and ceremony. Average cost: $250 to $500.

# ASK THE EXPERTS

**My parents want to hire a wedding consultant, and we have an appointment with someone who comes highly recommended from friends of the family. What should we expect at this first meeting?**

During your first meeting with a wedding planner, he or she will try to get to know you and your families and get a handle on your budget. It's important to be as open and honest as you can. Explain what your ideal wedding would be like, then fill her in on how much you have to spend and any family situations that may be pertinent. She'll explain the services she provides, and you can go from there.

**Where can I find a wedding planner?**

To find a coordinator in your area, contact the Association of Bridal Consultants (**www.bridalassn.com**, 860-355-0464).

**I feel funny hiring a stranger to help with my wedding. How can I get help without turning to a pro?**

Do you have any friends or family members who are very organized and did a superb job planning their own wedding recently? If so, consider asking her to be your unofficial wedding planner. You could pay her or tell her you would welcome her services in lieu of a gift.

# now what do I do?

## Answers to common questions

**My parents told me they can only give us $5,000 toward our wedding. Can we host a wedding on such a tight budget?**

You can have a small wedding on that budget if you spend wisely. Consider renting your church or synagogue hall for the reception. Visit local crafts shops during sales and pick up items to use for decorations. You'll probably have to pare down your guest list to the minimum, because 30 percent of a budget is usually spent on food and beverages. Since 30 percent of $5,000 is only $1,500, you won't have much to work with. You may wish to make some of the food yourselves, or enlist friends and family to help. Or why not have an afternoon ceremony followed by light hors d'oeuvres and a cake/champagne reception?

**We'd like a lavish wedding and plan to pay for some of it ourselves, with some help from my parents. Is it okay to ask my fiancé's parents to foot part of the bill?**

Sorry, but asking for money is never a good idea. However, if his parents have offered money for the wedding in the past, now is a good time to remind them about it and find out how serious they are. Be realistic when setting your wedding budget. This is just one day of your lives together, and whether you celebrate it with a $40,000 extravaganza or a $3,000 morning brunch, it's your marriage that's important.

**When we announced our engagement, my parents told us they'd give us $20,000 for a down payment on a house, as long as we have a very small wedding. Should we do this?**

That depends on what you want. Passing up the money for a down payment on a home is difficult. Are you currently in a position to make a down payment on your own? Do you need that money to stabilize your future together? If you don't, thank your parents and explain that you'd prefer to have a more lavish wedding celebration if they'd like to help fund it. In the end, the amount of money they offer must make both you and them comfortable.

**My aunt, who is also my godmother, doesn't have any children of her own. She would like to pay for my wedding gown and accessories. I think this is a beautiful gesture, but it bothers my mother. I don't want to hurt anyone's feelings. What should I do?**

Your aunt is very thoughtful, and I'm sure you're touched that she would like to give you this special gift for your wedding. Graciously accept her generosity. If your mom is still upset by this, talk with her about it. Remind her that your aunt will not be usurping her place in the wedding, just defraying the costs. Hopefully, after thinking about it your mom will understand and will be happy that your aunt loves you so much.

**How can we save money for our wedding?**

If you're paying for your wedding yourselves, consider having a set amount of money deducted from your paycheck each week, then having it deposited into a savings account. If both you and your fiancé put some money into the piggy bank each pay period, you'll have a nest egg to draw upon when those deposits and payments become due.

# Now WHERE DO I GO?!

**WEDDING PLANNERS AND SOFTWARE**

**The Designer Bride: A Wedding Planner and CD-ROM** by Janell Berté (**www.designerbride.com**, 717-291-9894)
This is one of the best wedding planners you'll find. The CD-ROM is packed with useful features, such as a guest-list organizer, a budget planner with tabs for multiple vendor estimates, and a gift-record database.

**BOOKS**

**Bridal Bargains: Secrets to Throwing a Fantastic Wedding on a Realistic Budget** by Denise and Alan Fields

**The Best Friend's Guide to Planning a Wedding: How to Find a Dress, Return the Shoes, Hire a Caterer, Fire the Photographer, Choose a Florist, Book a Band, and Still Wind Up Married at the End of It All** by Lara Webb Carrigan

**Budget Wedding Sourcebook** by Madeline Barillo

**Priceless Weddings for Under $5,000** by Kathleen Kennedy

**The Big Wedding on a Small Budget Planner & Organizer** by Diane Warner

**The Elegant Wedding and the Budget-Savvy Bride: How to Have the Wedding of Your Dreams for Half the Price** by Deborah McCoy

**The Complete Idiot's Guide to Budgeting for Your Wedding** by Sue Winner and Gerard J. Monaghan

During the hustle and bustle of wedding planning, it's easy to temporarily forget what all this commotion is really about: affirming a sacred bond between two people whose lives will now be intertwined as one. Carefully think about your wishes and desires, and create a ceremony that affirms your spiritual union.

# Planning Your Wedding Ceremony

# ceremony styles

**Suiting your needs**

*W*hat exactly is a wedding ceremony? Technically, it's the combination of readings and vows that makes your marriage "official" in the eyes of your community. Here, community can be anything from your immediate family to the members of your parish or synagogue. Following is a general outline of the elements that can make up a wedding ceremony:

**Processional** The musical prelude to which the official wedding party marches down the aisle. Depending on your tradition, music can be reserved just for the procession of the bride and her father or may include the mother of the bride and the groom's parents, as well as grandparents, bridesmaids, the flower girl, and ring bearer.

**Invocation** A welcome and initial prayer offered by the officiant (the person who marries you and your intended).

**Reading** The reading aloud of a passage from the Bible or other spiritual work.

**Vows** Promises you and your fiancé make to each other to affirm your love, respect, and commitment.

**Exchange of Rings** You and your beloved each place a wedding band on the other's left-hand ring finger.

**Intercession** A second short prayer or reading.

**Eucharist** The sharing of ritual bread and wine in some Christian religious services. It is not a required element of the ceremony, but many couples include it to symbolize their commitment to God.

**Nuptial Prayer** This is the biggie! This is when the officiant blesses the couple and pronounces you husband and wife!

**The Kiss** Nearly all ceremonies end with a kiss between the bride and groom.

**Recessional** The music that signifies the end of the ceremony.

## ASK THE EXPERTS

**How should we go about choosing an officiant?**

When choosing an officiant, make sure to speak with him or her in person before you make your decision. Ask yourself: Do you feel comfortable with him? Will he help you personalize your ceremony according to your needs and desires? Is he available on your wedding date? Is he open to letting you include your choice of readings, poems, and music? Will there be a sermon? Is any premarriage counseling required? Do you understand the fee for all services?

**Neither of us is affiliated with a house of worship. Who can we find to marry us?**

First, determine what type of wedding you want (religious, non-denomenational, civil, see pages 78-88 for more information). Get officiant recommendations from friends and relatives or simply look in the phone book or on the Internet.

## FIRST PERSON DISASTER STORY

## The Right Person for an Important Job

Neither of us was affiliated with a church, so we had to find an officiant. I figured one minister was the same as any other, so we booked the first one we found in the phone book. When we met to go over the details, he was very opinionated and gave us a list of readings that didn't reflect who we are as a couple, then gave us a sermon on political oppression. Our ceremony was okay but not what we had dreamed of. Whenever friends get engaged, we tell them to speak with several officiants and find one who will create a ceremony that suits them.

**Ann D., San Diego, California**

# catholic

**Celebrating the sacrament of marriage**

*F*or Catholics, marriage is considered one of the seven **sacraments**, Christian rites that signify spiritual divinity. And because marriage is a sacrament, it must take place within a Catholic church if it is to be considered sanctified (official) by the Roman Catholic Church.

A Catholic wedding ceremony is steeped in tradition and ritual, and few priests allow for variation. It usually opens with a musical prelude and processional, a welcoming prayer by your priest, and readings from the Bible, followed by a **homily** (a sermon by the priest about love and marriage). Next come **the rite of marriage** (the vows) and the exchange of rings. A nuptial Mass (the sharing of the Eucharist, or bread and wine) is optional—it adds about 20 minutes to the ceremony. The ceremony ends with the nuptial blessing.

To arrange a Catholic wedding, talk with your parish priest, who will want to meet with you and your fiancé. You will both need to present copies of your baptismal and confirmation certificates to show that each of you has been baptized and confirmed as a Catholic. Your priest will also ask some premarital questions to assure him of your intentions to follow the rules of the Church—for example, whether you attend Mass and will raise your children Catholic. He will ask that you sign up for Pre-Cana classes.

## ASK THE EXPERTS

**I'm Catholic and my fiancé is Protestant. Can we still get married in my church?**

Yes, but you will need to ask your priest for **dispensation** (approval from the Catholic Church to veer from their traditions). And your fiancé will have to agree to raise your children in the Catholic Church. Your priest applies for the dispensation on your behalf to the archbishop of his local diocese (religious district).

**I am a divorced Catholic. Can I get married in the church again?**

If you wish to be remarried in a Catholic church, you must seek an **annulment**—an official pronouncement from the Church stating that your first marriage was invalid. If you don't apply for an annulment or if one is not granted, then no, you may not remarry in a Catholic church.

# protestant

**From the
Book of Common Prayer**

*T*here are a lot of options for planning a Protestant wedding ceremony. The traditions will vary depending on whether you are Lutheran, Episcopalian, Methodist, Unitarian, Baptist, or Presbyterian. However, all denominations take the lead from the Book of Common Prayer.

A Protestant ceremony usually begins with the traditional processional, followed by a greeting offered by the minister. You may also choose a reading or two to be recited by your honor attendants before the minister gives a brief sermon. Then it's time for the vows, the exchange of rings, and possibly the lighting of a **unity candle** (a ritual involving the lighting of three candles. The mothers of the bride and groom each light one candle, then the bride and groom use those two candles to light their own candle together). The minister will then pronounce you husband and wife and will recite the nuptial blessing. At this point, the music plays and the recessional begins.

Speak with your minister about the specific rules and regulations followed by your particular house of worship.

 # ASK THE EXPERTS

**We are Lutheran. Will our minister give us strict guidelines for the ceremony, or do we have some creative leeway?**

At a Lutheran wedding ceremony, the minister is on hand solely as an official representative of the church and local government. He makes sure that you have fulfilled your obligations legally and with regard to your religion. Other than that, you can actually "marry" yourselves—meaning that you can write your own vows and select readings and music to make your ceremony unique. But don't worry, your minister will be available to guide you through the planning process and the wedding itself.

**I find the presenting of the bride by the father very patronizing. Is there any way around it?**

Yes. You can borrow a tradition often followed in Jewish marriage ceremonies in which both the mother and father walk the bride down the aisle and present her to the groom. Or you can walk down the aisle alone.

# jewish

**Mazel tov!**

*J*ewish marriage ceremonies are usually not held on the Sabbath (which lasts from sundown Friday until sundown Saturday), nor can they occur on any of the major Jewish holidays—the dates of which vary each year. Whether the ceremony takes place indoors or out, it is generally held under a **chuppah**, a canopy of cloth or flowers. The tradition of the chuppah is centuries old—it serves as a symbol of the new home the couple is about to enter. The bridal party stands under the canopy during the ceremony. Another unique Jewish tradition is the reading of the **ketubah**, or marriage contract, during the ceremony. In the olden days, the contract referred mainly to financial obligations, but today it includes vows of commitment and faith. Couples can write their own ketubah or use the traditional wording.

Unlike in traditional Christian ceremonies, the Jewish bride is escorted down the aisle by both parents. The height of the

**S**igning the ketubah (the Jewish marriage contract).

ceremony is the ring exchange. The seven wedding blessings—read in either English or Hebrew by your rabbi or honor attendants—end the actual ceremony. At the close of the service, it's customary for the groom to stomp on a glass and break it. The breaking of the glass signifies, among other things, that love and marriage are fragile and must be handled with care. Don't worry—even if your beloved is a klutz, he won't get hurt! The glass is usually safely tucked inside a decorated fabric bag or napkin.

## ASK THE EXPERTS

### Where do I get a chuppah?

Most caterers can rent you a chuppah. Another option is to have your florist create one out of flowers. Or simply buy some light-weight fabric and make your own. A typical chuppah is six feet square. Attach four poles (eight to 10 feet high) to each corner, and your chuppah is ready!

### How can we find an artist to create our ketubah or Jewish marriage contract?

Ask your rabbi, family, and friends for recommendations, or check out the following: The Artist's Wedding Studio, **www.chuppah.com** (631-537-8008); Our Jewish Company, **www.ketubah.com** (888-KETUBAH); and The Ketubah Gallery, **www.ketubahgallery.com** (888-884-3004).

### This seems silly, but it could be a problem. My fiancé did a trial run of the glass breaking, and he couldn't do it. What do we do at the ceremony if the glass doesn't break?

This can be a real problem, especially if you're getting married outdoors and your fiancé will be trying to break the glass on soft grass. Here's a simple trick that your rabbi will probably tell you: Since the glass is traditionally placed in a fabric bag, your guests never actually see it. You can substitute a lightbulb instead, which is much easier to break!

# interfaith

## Combining ideals

An interfaith marriage is one in which the bride and groom are of different religions. By coming together in marriage, both people have agreed to celebrate each other's beliefs, throughout their lives together as well as during their wedding ceremony.

When planning such a ceremony, you'll first have to educate your partner on the beliefs and traditions of your house of worship. Fill him or her in on the aspects you'd like to include in your wedding. For example, if you're Jewish, explain the significance of the chuppah, ketubah, and breaking of the glass. If you're Catholic, show your fiancé several traditional readings from the Bible.

Decide which elements you'd like to include, and piece together your own ceremony. It's important to include your spiritual guides (rabbi, priest, minister) in this process in order to help decide who will carry out certain parts of the ceremony. A word of caution: Not every religion embraces interfaith marriages. Speak with your clergy or rabbi to find out the stance of your house of worship and to determine what requirements must be met for your marriage to go forward.

When planning your interfaith ceremony, feel free to add newer symbolic gestures, such as a flower presentation to important family members or the giving of a family medallion (in the case of a second marriage when one or both parties already has children; see page 53).

# ASK THE EXPERTS

**My fiancé is Jewish and I'm Protestant. Can a rabbi and a minister both preside over our marriage?**

If you are planning an interfaith ceremony, it's a wonderful idea to have co-officiants. However, not many rabbis and ministers will accommodate such a request. Also, only one of them can officially sign your marriage certificate, so determine ahead of time who will be the "lead" officiant. That may dictate where the ceremony takes place.

**We saw an ad in a magazine for an officiant ordained by two different churches. Can he be genuine?**

Officiants who claim to be doubly ordained are not true representatives of any particular sect. Select another officiant or chose two different pastors to carry out your wishes.

**My fiancé was raised Baptist and I'm Catholic. We plan to have a nondenominational wedding. But what happens to our children—what religion will they have, if any?**

This is a good question to consider before you marry. You need to ask yourselves whether you feel that it's important for children to have a religious education. Even if you decide to raise them under one religion, know that most religions require the children themselves to confirm their beliefs, usually around the age of 12 or 13.

# nondenominational versus civil

## Spirituality is the difference

*W*hat exactly is a **nondenominational** ceremony? It's a ceremony that is performed by an officiant who is educated in all major religions and who can incorporate different elements that are comfortable for you and your fiancé. Nondenominational ministers attend to the spiritual needs of people no matter what religion they are, so this type of ceremony can be perfect for couples who don't belong to a house of worship. In addition, some couples wish to have a spiritual ceremony but not a religious one, which can also be performed by a nondenominational minister. And since there are no "rules of the road," your ceremony can take place just about anywhere, indoors or out.

A **civil ceremony,** on the other hand, does not include spiritual elements and is generally performed by a justice of the peace, judge, or a county or court clerk. This is the route to take if you want a ceremony without religious overtones. Since you can completely construct your event, you're free to use any literary works for your readings or even rock music for your processional and recessional. Civil ceremonies can take place at city hall, outdoors in a park or at your reception hall. (Nearly all elopements are civil ceremonies.) Discuss your options with your justice of the peace.

 ## ASK THE EXPERTS

**We'd like to be married on the beach by a nondenominational minister, but our families feel we should be married in a church, even though we don't belong to one. What should we do?**

For many couples, especially young couples, getting married marks their first official entry into adulthood. Not surprisingly, some parents may find it hard to accept this change in status and may insist that their children follow their parental wishes. Gently remind them that it is your wedding and that marrying in a church would make you uncomfortable. Your nondenominational minister can happily lend a sense of spirituality—as opposed to religion—to your ceremony. Speak with him to help determine what's best for you.

**Do you give a justice of the peace a gratuity?**

The fee for a civil ceremony ranges from $150 to $200, depending on the part of the country in which you live. And yes, you do tip the justice, usually anywhere from $25 to $50.

# the marriage license

## Filling out the paperwork

*B*efore you walk down the aisle, you and your fiancé need to apply for a **marriage license**. This document—issued by the city or town in which you'll be marrying—affirms that you're eligible to marry. Look in the phone book or call your local municipal offices to determine which department handles marriage licenses. In some cases you'll go to city hall, in others you'll report to the town clerk's office.

You and your fiancé must provide documentation to prove your identities and ages. Such official papers include certified copies of your birth certificates, proof of citizenship (such as passports) and driver's licenses. If you have been married before and are divorced, you'll need to provide the divorce decree; if your spouse passed away, you'll have to show the death certificate. Some states also require a **blood test**. Blood tests are used to screen for sexually transmitted diseases such as gonorrhea and syphilis, and in some states, tuberculosis. You will need to bring the lab report of your blood tests along as well.

At the town clerk's office, you will be given a license, which you will give to your officiant on the day of your wedding. Your officiant will sign the document and will return it to the marriage license bureau. You'll receive a certified copy of your marriage certificate within a few weeks.

| M78719020 | THE CITY OF NEW YORK<br>OFFICE OF THE CITY CLERK<br>MARRIAGE LICENSE BUREAU | License Number<br>M78719020 |
|---|---|---|

### Certificate of Marriage Registration

This Is To Certify That  Andrew Neilintz

residing at    30 2nd Avenue,  4A, New York, New York

born on     March 27,1975        at  Hartford, Connecticut  USA

and   Carole Lobara

residing at   19 1st Avenue, 24A, New York, New York

born on     March 25,1977        at  Flint, Michigan  USA

### Were Married

on  August 09,2000        at    MANHATTAN
1 CENTRE STREET, NEW YORK

# ASK THE EXPERTS

**Can we get our marriage license by mail?**

No, this isn't possible. You must apply together and in person and provide documents attesting to your identities and the fact that you are both free to marry. Some states may also require blood test results.

**We live in Baltimore, but we're getting married in Seattle. In which location do we apply for our marriage license?**

You need to apply for your marriage license in the town in which you'll be married. Call the city marriage license office and find out the particulars for that area. (How long is the license valid? Is there a waiting period? Is a blood test required? What days and times is the office open? Is an appointment necessary?) Then make plans to visit the office with your fiancé, and be sure to bring all of the necessary documents.

**I'd like to keep my own name after I'm married. Can I take care of that when I get my marriage license?**

How you fill out your marriage license will not affect your name. The form asks for the last names of both the bride and the groom. If you keep your surname, nothing changes. If you decide to change your name to your husband's, again, nothing changes on your license. After you are married, however, you will need to file a name change with your credit card companies, banks, etc. But first you will need to contact the department of motor vehicles (to change your driver's license) and the social security office (to get a social security card with your new, married name on it) and show them your marriage license. After you have your new driver's license and social security card, you can change your credit and bank cards without having to show them your marriage license.

# now what do I do?

## Answers to common questions

**We'd like to write our own vows. Where do we start?**

Wedding vows do two important things: They affirm your commitment to each other and they illustrate how that commitment will manifest in the future. To write your own vows, start by asking yourselves these questions: Why do you love each other? Why do you want to spend the rest of your lives together? What promises will you make to each other? Now write down your answers. Ideally, you want each of your answers to match in length. Next, copy your answers onto index cards and read them to each other. How does it feel to hear them? Edit as much or as little as you like. As the big day nears, copy your final version onto an index card—going blank in front of your friends and family is not the way you want to remember your ceremony! For more inspiration, get a copy of *The Knot's Guide to Wedding Vows and Traditions* by Carley Roney and *The Everything Wedding Vows Book* by Janet Anastasio.

**We're Catholic and want to marry in my parents' garden. Can our priest arrange this?**

If you're Catholic, you must marry in a church. While your priest can sometimes get a dispensation (approval to bend the rules), it can be difficult in some dioceses. Ask your parish priest about the possibility, but don't be surprised if the answer is no.

**My uncle is a minister at a Unitarian church, and he's offered to preside over our wedding. Can he act as our officiant, and can a family member sign our marriage certificate?**

As long as he is an ordained member of the clergy, there is no reason why he can't act as your officiant *and* sign your marriage certificate. If you have any doubts, double-check his officiant status at your local town clerk's office.

**We're Catholic, and we're getting married in my parish. I'd like to have both my parents walk me down the aisle. Is this possible?**

Ask your priest for permission. Explain why it is important for you to honor both your parents on your important day. Depending on your parish, you may be allowed to do it.

**Some churches are now insisting on premarital counseling. Is this new?**

Yes. A number of churches, including Lutheran and Baptist, are hoping that by requiring premarital counseling, they can cut down on the number of divorces. The Catholic Church has long required parishioners to attend group or private premarital counseling sessions with their priest. Some states, such as Florida, are even requiring residents to undergo such counseling before they can get their marriage license. In all cases, these states and churches hope the sessions will open a channel of communication between you and your fiancé about what each of you wants out of marriage. The more issues that are discussed prior to your getting married, the easier it will be to make tough decisions later.

##  NOW WHERE DO I GO?!

### BOOKS

**The Catholic Wedding Book**
by Molly K. Stein and William C. Graham

**Your Catholic Wedding:
A Complete Plan Book**
by Chris Aridas

**Annulment: A Step-by-Step Guide for
Divorced Catholics**
by Ronald T. Smith

**Annulment: Your Chance to Remarry
Within the Catholic Church**
by Joseph P. Zwack

**The Protestant Wedding Sourcebook:
A Complete Guide for Developing
Your Own Service**
by Sidney F. Batts

**The Complete Jewish Wedding Planner**
by Wendy Chernak Hefter

**The New Jewish Wedding**
by Anita Diamant

**Interfaith Wedding Ceremonies:
Samples and Sources**
by Joan C. Hawxhurst

**Celebrating Interfaith Marriages:
Creating Your Jewish/Christian
Ceremony**
by Devon A. Lerner

CHAPTER

# 6

The vows have been spoken, you're happily married . . . and now it's time to party! From designing your flowers to ordering the cake, here's everything you need to know about hosting your big celebration.

# The Reception

# your party style

**What makes you smile?**

*I*f the marriage ceremony is designed to strengthen your bond as a couple, then the reception exists to show the power of that new bond to the world and to celebrate it. After all, this is the first time you will be participating as husband and wife, and you'll want a reception that fits the occasion. What type of party do you envision? You may be dreaming of an elegant evening dinner party, the reception hall awash in the glow of candlelight. Or perhaps an afternoon garden party, featuring a his and hers softball game.

The important thing is to determine the style you are gravitating toward and then check out reception locations, entertainment, and decorations that will add to the theme. Think about weddings

or other celebrations you've been to in the past. What did you like about them? What aspects would you avoid?

Now is also the time to revisit your budget. How much did you allot for reception hall rental fees, food and beverages, wedding cake, music, limousines, flowers, invitations, photography, and videography? Keep these numbers in mind as you meet with vendors or wedding coordinators.

# ASK THE EXPERTS

**Help! I just finished finding the right dress, scheduling the church, and writing our vows. I don't think I can manage planning a reception too!**

Planning a wedding, from the engagement party to the honeymoon, is a big undertaking. Most brides tend to feel overwhelmed a few months into the process. Stop, take a moment and think about what you want. Do you want to micromanage your wedding yourself or hire someone to do that for you? Now may be the time to hire a wedding planner to help you prepare for your big day (see page 72). Or enlist the help of an organized friend.

**My fiancé is a drummer in a jazz trio. We're going to have a relaxed ceremony and a reception at the supper club where we met. It is so "us," but our families are not thrilled.**

Never let someone convince you to change the style of your wedding. If you love the idea of an intimate, relaxed party, just do it. Your families will realize that it's what's best for you, and they'll have a great time at the celebration no matter where it's held.

**I want to wear a traditional gown with a train and long gloves, but I'm afraid it may be too fancy to dance in at the reception.**

All gowns with trains include what is called a bustle. Basically, it's a system by which the train is gathered up and affixed to the skirt via buttons, hooks, or ribbons. In the end, your dress will be floor-length and you'll have no problem dancing. Just make sure your maid of honor or wedding coordinator knows how your bustle works and is on hand to help you get ready for the reception.

# reception sites

**A place to make memories**

As soon as you pick your wedding date, you should begin the hunt for the perfect reception location. Great sites are booked well in advance, so scout them out early. Make sure that you and your fiancé go on a site inspection for every location under consideration. And actually read—and understand—the terms of the contract before you sign on the dotted line. Here are other factors to consider when selecting a reception site:

- Is your preferred wedding date available?
- Does the site rental fee fit within your budget?
- What type of deposit is due and when? When is final payment due?
- Does the rental fee include a complimentary overnight hotel stay?
- How many hours does the rental fee cover?
- Are there separate setup and cleanup fees?
- Can the site accommodate the number of guests you wish to invite?
- Is the site close to your ceremony location?
- How many weddings will be hosted at this site on the same day?
- Can you select your own caterer or are meals created in-house?
- Can you hire an outside florist, baker, and musicians or is there a recommended list?
- Can you bring your own liquor?
- Will the site require a lot of decorations or is it beautiful as is?
- Is there adequate self-parking available for your guests? Is there a valet option?
- Is the site accessible for disabled or elderly guests?
- Are the restrooms easily accessible?
- Is the facility smoking/nonsmoking?

## ASK THE EXPERTS

**The reception hall we've chosen seemed to be a bargain, but we just received an itemized bill with all kinds of additional charges we weren't expecting.**

Many reception locations charge fees for various setup and cleanup activities. Before signing an agreement with any site, make sure you understand all the fees. And ask point-blank if there are any "hidden" fees.

**We've chosen a lovely inn for our ceremony and reception. The innkeepers want us to sign a contract and pay a 20 percent deposit now, with an agreement to pay the balance a month before the wedding. Is this standard?**

Yes. It's customary to pay a deposit to hold your wedding date. Many wedding service providers are in demand and can't hold dates without receiving partial payment. If you're worried that your vendors won't provide adequate services after you've paid, pay with a credit card instead of a personal check or cash. This way, if there are any disputes over services rendered, you'll have your credit card company standing behind you.

## FIRST PERSON — DISASTER STORY

### When it Rains, it Pours

We planned a lovely outdoor wedding at a banquet hall, but it rained, so we had to move the event indoors. We didn't think it would be a problem since we'd seen some of the hall's rooms, and they were beautiful. However, the room they put us in was a total disaster! The wallpaper was peeling, the carpet was stained and there were no windows! When we complained, the manager told us that this backup location was clearly explained in our contract. I wish we had read our contract more carefully and had demanded to see the rain-out location beforehand.

**Linda C., Philadelphia, Pennsylvania**

# caterer

**Give a memorable meal**

$\mathcal{T}$hink about some of the memorable parties you've attended. What stands out in your mind? The food, of course! Selecting the right caterer can make or break your wedding. And since food and beverage costs could take a 30 percent chunk out of your entire budget, who you choose to be your caterer is really an important financial decision as well.

If you're holding your reception at a hotel or banquet hall, chances are the caterer will be on-site, but sometimes you can hire an independent company. Speak with your banquet hall manager and find out the details. If you can hire an outside caterer, ask for recommendations of those that have worked the venue in the past.

Before you begin to meet with caterers, think about your wedding style again. Do you want a sit-down dinner or a buffet? Fancy fare or a country picnic? Picture your reception in your mind's eye, then describe it for the caterer. Of course, there are many questions you should ask potential caterers. Here are a few:

- Can you give me three references of couples who used your services recently?

- How many years have you been catering weddings?

- Do your chefs have a specialty or a signature menu?

- What is the price differential between a sit-down meal and a buffet?

- Can you provide special meals—for example, vegetarian?

- Are server gratuities included in the package price?

- Do you offer liquor and bartending services?

- What happens to leftover food?

- How much of a deposit is required and when?

- When is final payment due?

- Do you have a license and liability insurance?

# ASK THE EXPERTS

**We're Polish and have our hearts set on having traditional homemade pastries at our reception in addition to our wedding cake. We mentioned this to our caterer, and he told us we couldn't do it!**

Some caterers do require that any food served during your wedding come directly from them. Explain the situation to them: You're not doing this as a cost-cutting measure, but rather to add some ethnic touches. Perhaps the caterer will make an exception. If not, and if you haven't already signed a contract, you could always look for another caterer.

**We're trying to save money on our reception so that we can invite more people to our wedding. We're thinking about a simple afternoon event with passed hors d'oeuvres, wedding cake, and nonalcoholic punch. Will a caterer agree to such a menu?**

Of course. This is an elegant and cost-effective reception technique. Talk with your caterer and request several kinds of hors d'oeuvres. Make sure to pick some hot items and some cold. If you like, you can always augment the finger foods with a fruit and cheese platter.

# drinks

## Libation lessons

*T*he alcohol bill from any party can be hefty, so it's best to review all of your options beforehand. An **open bar** gives your guests unlimited access to beverages (alcoholic and non) for the duration of your reception. You are billed **on consumption,** or for the number of drinks that are served throughout the evening. (The bartenders keep track.) The average guest will drink three beverages in the first hour. Many caterers base the bar estimate on three drinks per person per hour. Be sure to decide how long you want the bar to remain open.

At a **cash bar,** your guests pay for their own drinks. This is not appropriate at a wedding reception. When speaking with your caterer or banquet manager, ask for a price breakdown between **house brand** (generic brands) and **premium brand** (upscale) drinks before you make your decision.

If cost is an issue, consider serving only beer, wine, and soft drinks, but not mixed drinks. Or opt for a festive signature drink, such as punch (it can also be nonalcoholic).

Your reception hall manager will fill you in on their guidelines and let you know what time last call will be.

### Peter Morrell's Selects for Champagne

**AMERICAN**
Domaine Chandon Brut
Napa Valley, California
$15 to $16

Mumm Curvée Napa
Napa Valley, California
$14 to $16

**FRENCH**
Perrier-Jouët Brut
$25 to $30

Möet and Chandon Brut Imperial
$30 to $40

From Peter Morrell's
**Barnes & Noble Basics** *Wine*

# ASK THE EXPERTS

**How many people does a bottle of champagne serve?**

Champagne is often served when toasting the bride and groom, usually after the speech by the best man (see page 162). The rule of thumb is six glasses per one bottle. A party of 100 people would require 17 bottles for one toast. Order extra to be safe.

**Our caterer is suggesting that we not serve champagne with our wedding cake. Why?**

Many people pair champagne with wedding cake, but it is not an ideal match because champagne is dry and wedding cake is sweet. Because champagne is a "high acid" wine, it does not go well with foods that are sweet and rich. Your caterer is right to suggest instead serving a dessert wine, such as a sauternes. But tradition is strong and most brides opt for champagne anyway.

**We're having a morning wedding, so our cocktail hour will begin at 10:30 a.m. That's awfully early to start serving alcohol, isn't it?**

It is a bit early for cocktails, but you can serve mimosas (champagne mixed with orange juice) or Bloody Marys (tomato juice and vodka), drinks that are traditionally served with brunch. Once your luncheon begins you could have waiters place wine on the tables or open a bar for mixed drinks and beer.

**We want to serve only white wine at our reception. How many bottles will we need for 150 people?**

You'll need about 40 bottles. The standard rule is four people per bottle of wine. The good news is that you should be able to get a discount if you buy the wine by the case.

# wedding cakes

**One piece is never enough**

𝒜 wedding cake serves as both a sweet ending to a wonderful meal and a work of art decorating your reception site. Talented bakers can create masterpieces out of sugar, flour, and eggs. Make an appointment with your baker to review your options. He'll most likely start off by telling you about any specialties he may have. Then you'll be able to flip through his portfolio of wedding-cake photos.

It's best to come to this first meeting with a few photos of wedding cakes that you like to help your baker steer you toward the right cake. Look for examples in bridal magazines or pick up a book devoted to these culinary masterpieces.

Once you have a basic design in mind, decide what flavor cake and filling you'd like. How about selecting a yellow cake with a Bavarian cream filling? Perhaps you'd prefer chocolate cake with Chambord mousse and fresh raspberries? Many couples opt for white cake with a Grand Marnier mousse filling. As for the icing on the cake, you have multiple options. Basic **butter cream** is light, creamy and delicate with a sweet buttery taste. **Fondant** icing is actually a sugar paste that is rolled out with a rolling pin, then applied over the cake for a perfectly smooth, satinlike finish. It tastes rich and sweet and has a doughy consistency. For decorations, your baker can use fresh flowers, butter-cream accents, spun sugar decorations, or rolled fondant ribbons and bows.

 # ASK THE EXPERTS

**My fiancé loves cheesecake. Is it possible for a baker to create a traditional-looking wedding cake out of several layers of cheesecake?**

There are many bakers who specialize in wedding cheesecakes. Ask your family and friends for local recommendations. Then give the bakers a call to find out if they can create what you want.

**We've heard that many couples save a piece of their wedding cake, freeze it, and eat it on their first anniversary. Does the cake taste okay after all that time?**

Actually, it's not really a good idea to eat anything that's been frozen for more than two or three months. Many couples still follow this tradition, but the cake usually ends up freezer-burned and tasteless. Instead, enjoy the cake at your reception.

**How much will a wedding cake cost?**

That depends on where you live, the type of cake you've chosen, and how many people it will serve. Some bakers require a minimum order—in other words, a cake that feeds 50 (even if you don't have that many guests). Other bakers will create a cake that serves the needs of your guest list. In general, you can expect to pay between $3 and $12 per slice of wedding cake, and intricate designs may cost even more.

# music

Dance the
night away

For some, a wedding just isn't a wedding without a mirrored ball, dance floor, and a funky D.J. If that's what your heart desires, start auditioning D.J.'s now. You can ask for a video demo of their services, or try catching them live at another event. Other couples prefer live musicians, such as a jazz trio, calypso band, or small orchestra. Speak with vendors, then compare the price quotes with your budget. To find musicians in your area, ask friends and family for recommendations, look in bridal magazines, and contact the American Federation of Musicians (**www.afm.org**, 212-869-1330). Or if you can't afford professional musicians, call a local music college and ask if any of their students would like to audition for your event.

Whether choosing a D.J. or a band, find out who in the band will be the **master of ceremonies.** His job is to announce the bridal party, begin the first dance, introduce any toasters (see page 162) and make sure the entertainment portion of the evening goes smoothly. Make sure to give him all the details of your event, including the names of everyone in the wedding party.

Most bands take a short break every hour. While at first this may seem daunting, it lets your guests take a break from the dance floor to rest and eat. You are usually required to feed the band, so add them to your head count. However, it's perfectly fine to feed them deli sandwiches rather than the full-scale reception meal. If you're concerned about the lull in entertainment, ask the reception venue if they can pipe in background music during the breaks, or set up a CD player.

# First Song Ideas for Your Wedding Reception

## TRADITIONAL

1. All of Me (Marks/Simons/Simons)
2. An Affair to Remember - Our Love Affair (Adamson/McCarey/Warren)
3. At Last (Gordon/Warren)
4. Can't Help Falling in Love (Creatore/P/W)
5. Chances Are (Allen/Stillman)
6. Embraceable You (Gershwin)
7. Isn't It Romantic (Hart/Rodgers)
8. It Had to Be You (Jones/Kahn)
9. Lovely - Just the Way You Look Tonight (Fields/Kern)
10. Misty (Burke/Garner)
11. My Funny Valentine (Hart/Rodgers)
12. Only You (Ram/Rand)
13. Love Is Here to Stay (Gershwin/Gershwin )
14. Smoke Gets in Your Eyes (Harbach/Kern)
15. Someone to Watch Over Me (Gershwin/Gershwin)
16. The Shadow of Your Smile (Mandel/Webster)
17. The Very Thought of You (Noble)
18. Unchained Melody (North/Zaret)
19. Unforgettable (Gordon)
20. When I Fall in Love (Heyman/Young)

## CONTEMPORARY

1. Annie's Song (Denver) — John Denver
2. Because You Loved Me (Warren) — Céline Dion
3. Butterfly Kisses (Carlisle/Thomas) — Jeff Carson
4. Endless Love (Richie) — Lionel Richie
5. First Time Ever I Saw Your Face (Maccoll) — Roberta Flack
6. For You (Lerum) — Kenny Lattimore
7. From This Moment On (Lange/Twain) — Shania Twain
8. Grow Old With Me (Lennon) — Mary Chapin Carpenter
9. Have I Told You Lately That I Love You (Morrison) — Rod Stewart
10. Here and Now (Elliot/Steele) — Luther Vandross
11. Hero (Afanasieff/Carey) — Mariah Carey
12. Just the Two of Us — Bill Withers
13. Just the Way You Are (Joel/Williams) — Billy Joel
14. Ribbon in the Sky (Wonder) — Stevie Wonder
15. Theme From Ice Castles - Looking Through the Eyes of Love (Hamlisch/Sager)
16. They Long to Be Close to You (Bacharach/David) — Carpenters
17. Wind Beneath My Wings (Henley/Silbar) — Bette Midler
18. You Are So Beautiful (Fisher/Preston) — Joe Cocker
19. You Light Up My Life (Brooks) —Debbie Boone
20. Your Song (John/Taupin) — Elton John

## FIRST DANCE

For your first dance, select a song that is meaningful to both of you. It's a good idea to practice dancing to it a few times before the wedding. After you've danced together, you and the closest male member of your family, usually your dad, will share a dance, followed by your groom and his closest female relative, such as his mom. Another event that you may want to have a special musical accompaniment to is the garter toss (see page 161).

# transportation

**Limos, cars,
and carriages**

*G*etting everyone to the church on time is actually a lot harder than you'd think. That's why it can be a good idea to provide transportation for everyone in the bridal party. You may use your own vehicles or select limousines, town cars, vintage cars, horse-drawn carriages, or even old VW Bugs to ferry everyone around. The important thing is to pick a mode of transportation that you'll enjoy, that you can afford, and that will get all of you there on time.

When calling transportation providers, ask about their vehicles (make, model, age, color), hourly rates, discounts for multiple rentals, and payment plans. If you're hiring a limousine, ask if champagne is included or if you'll have to stock the interior bar yourselves. Ask about backup transportation in case the vehicle(s) you rent break down or don't show up at all.

Next, carefully map out a schedule of the day. Make sure everyone in the bridal party is aware of the pickup times and ask them to be prompt. Just a five-minute delay at each stop could cause quite a snag at the ceremony.

To find a reputable limousine service in your area, contact the National Limousine Association (**www.limo.org**, 800-652-7007). For horse-drawn carriages, contact the Carriage Association of America (**www.caaonline.com**, 856-935-1616).

# ASK THE EXPERTS

**We hired limousines to take the bridal party from our home to the ceremony and then to the reception. We'd prefer not to incur the expense of having the limos return later. How should we get the bridal party home?**

Consider renting less-expensive town cars or a minibus for the bridal party's return trip. Your can also ask other guests to offer rides to the bridal party, but that could be tricky, depending on when everyone chooses to leave the reception.

**What if the limo doesn't show up on our big day?**

This is a common concern, and it has happened on occasion. Reconfirm your scheduled pickup time a week before the wedding and again the day before. Make sure you have the rental company's phone number handy, as well as an emergency number. About an hour before your scheduled pickup time, call the company to reconfirm one last time. It's also a good idea to have a backup plan just in case, which may be as simple as hopping in your car.

**We have several out-of-town guests flying in for the wedding. Are we responsible for providing their transportation from the hotel to the wedding?**

No, you aren't obligated to provide transportation, but do everything you can to make it easy on your guests. Before the wedding, give them information on local car-rental agencies and taxis, and provide a detailed map with directions from the airport to their hotel and from the hotel to the wedding site. Go an extra step and include directions for getting back to the hotel, too.

# flowers

Living decor

$\mathscr{B}$efore meeting with florists in your area—remember to get recommendations first—look in bridal magazines and books for samples that you like. Armed with those sample photos, you're ready to begin. Before you start on your flower selection, tell your florist exactly how many bouquets and boutonnieres will be needed, whether chair bows and floral garlands will be necessary at the ceremony, and how many tables there will be at the reception.

It's important to trust the florist you are working with and to be able to ask for his advice. If you're hosting an outdoor wedding in mid-July, ask which flowers will stand up to the heat all day and look fresh in photos. Likewise, if yours is a winter wedding, be sure your flowers can stand a bit of cold air. For those who are very budget-conscious, ask your florist to use local buds that are in season to avoid high import charges.

Aside from your bouquet, you'll also need to think about ordering flowers for the following:

- A bouquet for each bridesmaid
- Corsages for mothers and grandmothers
- Boutonnieres for groom, ushers, fathers, grandfathers, ring bearers
- Basket of flowers for the flower girl
- Flower arrangements for the chapel or chuppah
- Pew flowers and/or bows, aisle runners
- Centerpieces for each reception table
- Decor flowers for the gift table and the wedding cake table

# ASK THE EXPERTS

**Which flowers are in season in the spring and summer?**

Here's a basic list of the flowers that thrive locally during the various seasons:

| All Year | Spring/Summer | Fall/Winter |
|---|---|---|
| Calla Lily | Anemone | Amaryllis |
| Carnation | Aster | Bells of Ireland |
| Casablanca Lily | Cosmos | Bird of Paradise |
| Delphinium | Daffodil | Calendula |
| Dendrobium Orchid | Dahlia | Cattleya Orchid |
| Eucalyptus | Daisy | Chrysanthemum |
| Freesia | Forget-me-not | Heather |
| Gardenia | Hyacinth | Holly |
| Gerbera Daisy | Iris | Hydrangea |
| Lily of the Valley | Jasmine | Phlox |
| Phalaenopsis Orchid | Lilac | Poppy |
| Queen Anne's Lace | Narcissus | Star of Bethlehem |
| Rose | Peony | Sunflower |
| Snapdragon | Rose | Sweet William |
| Stargazer Lily | Sweet Pea | Violet |
| Stephanotis | Tulip | |

# photographer

## Capturing the moment

*Y*our photographer will be the memory keeper of your very special day. Be sure to research and find the right one for you. To locate a photographer in your area, ask friends and family for references. When you get a few names, call and make sure the photographer has shot a number of weddings. You want someone familiar with the ins and outs of weddings so that he won't miss any key moments.

Questions to ask your prospective photographer:

- Does the photographer shoot in color, black and white, or both? Does he shoot 35mm, medium format, or both?

- Will he or an assistant be shooting your wedding? Know exactly who is going to shoot your wedding, and ensure that you're looking at *his* or *her* portfolio. If dealing with a one-person operation, find out who would cover your wedding in case of an emergency.

- How does the photographer determine price? There are several ways: by the number and kinds of prints you think you'll want, by the number of rolls of film he shoots, by the hours he spends at your wedding, or a combination thereof. Ask him how many rolls of film will be shot and how many proofs and final prints will result. Inquire about discount packages.

- Does the photographer develop his own film? Can you buy your negatives from him? Do you get to see paper proofs, or can he show you proofs on video or CD-ROM or via e-mail?

- Be sure you like his style. Can you tolerate his presence throughout the entire day? You should feel very comfortable around your photographer. If not, rest assured it will show in your wedding album!

# ASK THE EXPERTS

**Should I tell my photographer what to shoot?**

Absolutely. On average, a traditional photographer will photograph 200 to 300 images of a wedding. Make sure some of those are the ones you really want. Write down a list of your desired shots and their locations. If you are having a sit-down lunch or dinner, it's a good idea to include a shot of each table.

**What is the difference between traditional wedding photography and photojournalism?**

According to Jeff Hawkins (**www.jeffhawkins.com**), well-known photojournalist, this is the answer: "Wedding photojournalism is the art of capturing the wedding as it happens, rather than creating it. You end up with storybooks, not the traditional wedding album. Your friends and family can look back on the day and feel the laughter, the tears, and the joy. **Photojournalism** is capturing the details, the emotions, and the feelings in an unobtrusive style. It's anticipating the images before they happen and adding an artistic edge.

Whereas traditional photography is capturing the posed groupings and only the important events such as the cake cutting and the bouquet toss, this style differs. On an average, a traditional photographer will photograph 200 to 300 images of a wedding day. However, a wedding photojournalist will typically photograph between 500 and 700 images per wedding. However, many of our weddings have gone over 1,000, the most being in excess of 1,400."

Jeff Hawkins

# videographer

**Moving pictures**

*A* videographer captures your wedding day as it unfolds. Some professionals simply give you the straight-ahead raw footage, while others do extensive postproduction work, adding stills of your wedding invitation and family photos as well as a musical score.

As with a wedding photographer, ask recently married brides for recommendations of a videographer. Before you meet with any, ask to view a demo tape. Ideally, he or she will have shot footage at your wedding location already or at least have tapes from similar affairs.

When viewing a demo tape, look for the following:

- Sharp focus
- Close-ups when appropriate
- Clear audio
- Smooth transitions
- Titles and special effects (but not overdone)

## INTERVIEW WITH THE EXPERT / Videographer

**Mark LeGrand**
**Pro One Video** (www.proonevideo.com)

"Don't forget to ask what type of equipment will be used. A professional videographer will use broadcast-quality—or three-chip—cameras, wireless microphones, and professional lighting. The videographer's editing system is also very important, since at least 50 percent of your tape involves editing in postproduction."

# ASK THE EXPERTS

**We've seen many demos from various videographers. Is it okay to ask for a sample of an actual wedding video?**

That's a great idea. After all, a demo may just be bits and pieces of the best wedding clips they've ever done. Once you've seen the demo and a whole wedding video, you should be prepared to make your decision.

**Many videographers have suggested that we go for a package with two cameras at the ceremony.**

If you can afford the extra camera, go for it. That's because two cameras can more effectively capture all the emotions during the ceremony. One camera can focus on the bride and groom up close and personal. The second camera can take wide shots of the event, which can then be edited in with the close-ups later. Also, many officiants don't allow videographers to move around for fear of disrupting the ceremony.

**What is a three-chip camera?**

Three-chip cameras are broadcast-quality and create images by filtering the three primary colors individually. The colors are then combined to create a video signal with sharp colors. Most professional photographers will use this type of equipment.

# invitations

Find your
stationery style

*Y*ou have a lot of options when it comes to invitations. Depending on your wedding style, there are four basic types of invitation printing to choose from:

- **Engraved invitations** are very formal, elegant, and expensive. This is because the wording is actually etched onto a steel plate, which is then inked. Fine cotton paper is used with this method because it will readily accept the ink and leave the letters raised a bit off the paper.

- Though less expensive than engraving, **thermography** yields similar quality. The key is in the ink, which contains a special powder. When heated, the ink rises a bit and becomes shiny.

- Most couples today tend to opt for offset **lithography**, because of its cost-effectiveness and speedy delivery times. Offset printing starts with a flexible plate that contains your invitation wording. It is inked, and the image is then transferred onto paper.

- Finally, you can use **laser printing** to create your own invitations. While the lettering will appear crisp, it won't provide the rich, raised look of engraving. Laser printers use an electrostatic charge to transfer images onto paper.

## Invitation Time Line

*A*bout six months before your wedding, you should select an invitation style that matches the tone of your event. Three or four months prior to the event, you should place your order. (Make sure to order enough invitations. If you run out and need two or three more, you'll have to pay a fortune for a minimum order of 25.) Hire a calligrapher to address your envelopes or do it yourself. Six to eight weeks before your wedding, go to the post office and have one invitation envelope weighed. Purchase the necessary stamps and mail the invitations. The RSVP date on your cards should be three weeks before your wedding date.

# ASK THE EXPERTS

**We are having a large, traditional wedding. The stationer suggested the following: an invitation card with a tissue-paper covering, a card announcing the time and location of the reception, an RSVP card and envelope, a map with directions from the ceremony to the reception, and an inner envelope for the entire package. Can we drop any of these items to save a bit of money?**

If your ceremony and reception will take place in the same spot, consider skipping the reception card. And if your guests are all locals familiar with the area, don't bother with the map, or supply it yourself.

**We visited a stationery store and selected our invitations. Later that week, I went to a party supply store and saw the same invitations for less money!**

Remember that a major component of ordering your invitations from a stationer is customer service. A professional who deals with wedding invitations can help you select the right style and wording and ensure that you follow standard traditions. He may also know which ink colors will highlight your color scheme and fit into your overall wedding vision. At discount retailers, invitation albums are left out on a table, and you help yourself in a self-service manner. If you know exactly what you want and how to word your invitation, this discount method may be for you. Mail-order catalogs and Web sites also offer lower-cost ordering.

# now what do I do?

## Answers to common questions

**We don't want to hire a professional photographer. Instead, we're thinking of asking my uncle to take the pictures.**

Ask yourselves why you don't want to hire a photographer. Is it too expensive? Are you uncomfortable having your picture taken? If you can isolate the reason why you don't want to hire someone, you may be able to find a professional who is willing to meet your needs. Having a family member take photos can backfire on you. The person may feel stuck behind the camera all day and not be able to enjoy your special event. Something may go wrong with the equipment, resulting in bad feelings—and no photos!—after the fact. If you can, hire a cost-effective photographer, or at the very least, a photography student from a local college.

**Should we order thank-you notes from the same stationer who provided our invitations?**

You can, but it will be expensive. A better idea is to order cards with only your names printed on them. You can use them for thank-you notes as well as other correspondence you will have as a couple. And since newlyweds often move after their first year of married life, don't purchase addressed envelopes.

**We'd like to chose an unusual reception location. Where should we look?**

Start here: American Association of Botanical Gardens and Arboreta (**www.aabga.org**, 610-925-2500), Art Museum Network (**www.amn.org**), National Historic Landmarks (**http://cr.nps.gov/nhl/**), National Park Service (**www.nps.gov**, 202-208-6843), and the National Trust for Historic Preservation (**www.nationaltrust.org**).

**We love the idea of a wedding cake as art and plan to spend a big chunk of our budget on the cake. Where can we get some ideas?**

To gather ideas, look at magazines, books, and Web sites. Some well-known pros include:
Sylvia Weinstock Cakes (**www.sylviaweinstockcakes.com**, 212-925-6698),
Colette's Cakes (**www.colettescakes.com**, 212-366-6530),
Ron Ben-Israel Cakes (**www.weddingcakes.com**, 212-625-3369),
Gail Watson Cake (**www.gailwatsoncake.com**, 212-967-9167),
Cake Diva (**www.cakediva.com**, 212-722-0678), and
Rosebud Cakes (**www.rosebudcakes.com**, 310-657-6207).

**I'd like to make my own bouquet and centerpieces. Where can I buy flowers in bulk?**

This is a great option if you have the time and talent to do it. Contact the following sellers for more information: 2G Roses (**www.freshroses.com**, 800-880-0735), **GreatFlowers.com** (800-360-9193), and Farmfresh Flowers (**www.farmfreshflowers.com**, 877-376-3774).

**What are some sources for unusual invitations?**

For unique handmade and do-it-yourself invitations, contact Kate's Paperie (**www.katespaperie.com**, 212-633-0570), **Invitesite.com** (626-584-9804), Individual Papers (**www.individualpapers.com**, 401-738-2525), A Wedding Invitation (**www.aweddinginvitation.com**, 888-644-2273), and Dahlia Invites (**www.dahliainvites.com**, 866-340-4440).

# NOW WHERE DO I GO?!

## CONTACTS

Jeff Hawkins Photography
(**www.jeffhawkins.com**, 407-834-8023)

Wedding & Event Videographers Association International
(**www.weva.com**, 941-923-5334)

Wedding and Portrait Photographers International
(**www.wppi-online.com**, 310-451-0090)

## BOOKS

**The Perfect Wedding Reception: Stylish Ideas for Every Season**
by Maria McBride-Mellinger and Siobhan McGowan

**Beverly Clark's Book of Wedding Cakes**
by Beverly Clark

**Colette's Wedding Cakes**
by Colette Peters

**The Wedding Cake Book**
by Dede Wilson

**Bridal Flowers: Arrangements for a Perfect Wedding**
by Maria McBride-Mellinger

**Flowers: For Your Wedding**
by Tracy Guth

**Bouquets: A Year of Flowers for the Bride** by Marsha Heckman

CHAPTER

*7*

There's nothing quite like the feeling you get the first time you put on a wedding gown. Selecting the dress somehow makes the entire event finally seem real. This is your moment to shine! You and your fiancé are the stars of this show, and you'll want to dress the part.

# Gowns and Formal Wear

# the wedding gown

## A princess in white

**A**

$\mathscr{F}$inding the right dress is a challenge. For some, the moment they put on that special dress, it's a fairy tale come true; for others, it's a decision nightmare. Relax and take a deep breath. You found the right man—the dress is secondary.

Before you start shopping, get an idea of what you want. Purchase the latest issues of bridal magazines such as *Modern Bride* and *Bride's*. Tear out pictures of the gowns you like and start a clippings file. Search the Internet. The Knot's (**www.theknot.com**) dress guide allows you to search by price, designer, color, or style attributes (see sleeves and necklines below), and you can keep an online "notebook" of dresses.

Next, find the best wedding gown stores near you by asking friends and family for recommendations. There are two types of stores to

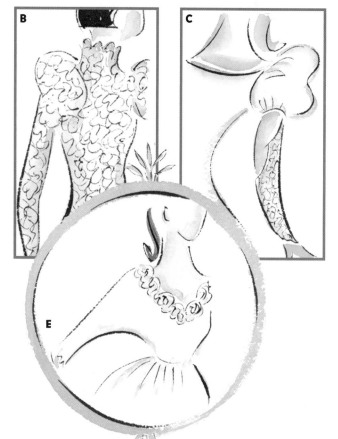

**A** Sweetheart neckline with leg o'mutton sleeve

**B** Collar band with Juliet-style sleeve

**C** Bateau neckline with gaunlet sleeve

**D** Portrait neckline with fitted-point sleeve

**E** Décolletage neckline with dolman sleeve

consider: full-service and discount. **Full-service bridal shops** usually require you to make an appointment; the same goes for the bridal departments of large department stores. When you arrive, a salesperson will probably make recommendations based on your body type. Now is a good time to bring out your clippings. While some stores let you browse their racks, others whisk you into a dressing room and bring the gowns they choose for you. Either way, these gowns are samples (expect to see some wear and tear and makeup stains). Chances are, they won't even have your size. When you find the right gown style, you will be measured and an order in your size will be placed.

**Discount wedding stores** let you browse and try on as many dresses as you like. You can buy your dress off the rack if it fits or place an order. Many of these shops don't carry brand-name designers but instead carry their own labels. Some discount stores have seamstresses who can make any necessary alterations.

 ## ASK THE EXPERTS

### What's the average price of a wedding gown and veil?

The average price of a gown is about $800 and $100 for a veil. That said, designer gowns can cost anywhere from $2,000 to $10,000, while discount labels sell wedding gowns for under $500.

### I just picked up my wedding gown, and after I tried it on, I found I really don't like it after all. What can I do?

In most cases, once you've ordered a wedding gown, you're stuck. That's because most wedding gowns are sold as special orders only. In other words, the shop orders a particular dress in your exact size from the gown manufacturer. While every store is different, you can expect to pay a deposit of one-third or one-half, or even the entire amount of the dress. If you refuse the dress, then you lose your deposit. Try talking with the store manager. She may be willing to restock the dress and allow you to select something else. (Of course, if the dress is damaged or the wrong size or color, the fault lies with the store.)

# nontraditional wedding attire

**Making an impression**

*N*ot every couple goes the traditional route when it comes to wedding-day attire. There's no law that says you must spend megabucks on a white wedding gown or that your groom has to wear a tuxedo. Wear what you want, but make sure it's in keeping with the overall style of your wedding.

Where to find this special dress? Try the evening-wear section of your favorite department store. For a less formal look, try a gently tailored suit or a simple, inexpensive afternoon tea dress.

## FIRST PERSON DISASTER STORY

### Ten Pounds Later

I was so ecstatic to find the perfect gown so early on in my search. I ordered it in my size, and when it arrived, a month before my wedding, it fit like a dream. One less thing to think about, or so I thought. While it sat in my closet, I was tearing around town interviewing bands and photographers, to say nothing of holding down my real-life job as a real-estate broker. Two days before my wedding, I put on my gown, only to find that it was hanging on me. Apparently I had lost 10 pounds and hadn't even realized it! My mom and I made a frantic search for a seamstress who could tighten up the bodice. In the end, we used safety pins and no one knew. I didn't realize that you're supposed to try on your gown a few days before the big day for just these kinds of emergencies. My mom and I still joke about my bridal diet.

**Liz T., Miami, Florida**

Veils can pose a problem for the nontraditional dress. Consider tipping your veil to your ethnic heritage: a red veil for a Chinese ceremony or black lace for a Spanish wedding. For those of you from the British Isles, why not have your groom and ushers wear kilts? Theme attire—such as medieval, Renaissance, Victorian, or western—can also make a lasting impression if your event has been planned accordingly (see pages 48-49). When choosing what to wear on your big day, just remember to be creative and have fun!

## ASK THE EXPERTS

**I'd like to design my own gown and have it made for me. Will that be really expensive?**

The cost of a self-designed gown depends on several factors: the seamstress you hire, the type of fabric you choose and the complexity of the design. Take your sketch to several local seamstresses and talk about your gown. Get a solid price quote from each person and ask to see samples of their work. Go with the person you feel most comfortable with. Just make sure to check their references before paying your deposit. In the case of a handmade gown, you will probably have to pay for the materials first, as well as making a nonrefundable deposit, so be sure this is the direction you want to go in.

**My mom wants to sew my wedding dress. Where do we find bridal gown patterns?**

Go to your local fabric store and look through pattern books found at most fabric stores. Each pattern company, such as Vogue, Butterick, and McCalls, offers several wedding gown designs. If you don't find one pattern that fits your needs, purchase several and piece the gown together. Combine the sleeve style from pattern A, the neckline from pattern B, and the skirt design from pattern C. That way you'll be able to further customize your dress.

# dressing the ladies

**Bridesmaids, mothers, and flower girls**

What the bridal party wears should highlight the style—and any underlying theme—of your wedding. While some brides let their bridesmaids chose what they want, most pick the style of gown for their attendants. It's also popular for the bride to choose a particular color and then have each individual bridesmaid choose a gown in that color in the style that best suits her. Keep in mind your attendants' body types—and the size of their wallets—when selecting a dress style, and make sure it is appropriate for all of your bridesmaids. If you are having junior bridesmaids (children between the ages of 7 and 15), it's customary that they wear dresses similar to those of the bridesmaids, just not as fancy.

When ordering bridesmaids gowns as a group, it's very important to place one order so that each dress is cut from the same dye lot of fabric. Otherwise, you run the risk of there being slight color variations between the dresses. When purchasing from many bridal designers, it can take up to three months for gown delivery. Make sure you know the time frame before you put down a deposit. Some designers, such as Alfred Angelo, offer their popular styles with a "quick ship" option. Alternatively, stores such as David's Bridal offer off-the-rack bridesmaids dresses—a great solution if you're in a time crunch.

Dresses for moms can get pricey too, so don't forget to check out the selection of special-occasion gowns at department stores or through mail-order catalogs. J.C.Penney (**www.jcpenney.com**, 800-222-6161) offers a catalog exclusively for wedding parties that features discounted dresses from many designers, including Alfred Angelo, Sweetheart, and Jessica McClintock. You can also check out Chadwick's of Boston (**www.chadwicks.com**, 800-246-4462) and Talbot's (**www.talbots.com**, 800-882-5268) for more ideas.

# ASK THE EXPERTS

**My bridesmaids are complaining that the gown I chose for them is unflattering. What should I do?**

If your bridesmaids have widely varying body shapes, it may be difficult to select one gown that looks good on everyone. Consider a simple A-line style, which looks good on everyone no matter how tall or short, plump or slender. Another idea is to let your bridesmaids choose their own dress style, provided they're made from the same fabric or at least share the same color. That way, there will be some continuity among your bridesmaids but each will wear something that is flattering to her figure.

**My mother-in-law wants to wear an off-white dress to my wedding. I think that's really crass. What should I do?**

If your mother-in-law's choice of an off-white dress bothers you, let her know—but tread gently. While this is *your* big day, it is also a big day for her. Send someone from your wedding party to talk to her about it—for example, your maid of honor. She simply may not realize your concern and may be more than happy to get her dress in another color. If she resists getting a new dress, let it roll off your back. On your wedding day, no one will be looking at your mother-in-law because all eyes will be on you.

# tuxedos

## Men in black

*Imagine* this: The doors of the chapel fly open, you begin to walk down the aisle, and you catch your first glance of your husband-to-be, dressed in his tuxedo finery. You're swept off your feet all over again!

The groom, both fathers, and the ushers traditionally wear tuxedos to the wedding. A tux is comprised of a coat, pants, shirt, neckwear (tie or bow tie), cummerbund, vest, handkerchief, shoes, and socks. Most men don't own a tux, so you'll need to find a reputable rental agency in your area. Luckily, there is no shortage of service providers in this arena.

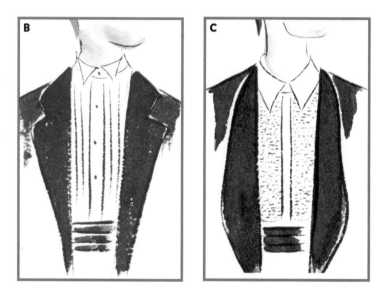

**A** Peak lapel
**B** Notch lapel
**C** Shawl lapel

If the bride and bridesmaids are going to wear elaborate gowns, then only tuxedos will do. There are three basic styles to choose from based on the collar design. You can choose a shawl, notch, or peak collar. Each of these jacket types can be rented as single- or double-breasted. Your rental specialist will help your groom determine the best style for him and his ushers.

 ## ASK THE EXPERTS

**Our ushers live in several different states. How should we rent tuxedos?**

If you've got groomsmen traveling in from other locations, the easiest thing is to select a tux style in your own hometown. Then ask the rental agent if they have measurement forms you can send to your ushers. Many national tuxedo chains allow groomsmen to visit a local shop and be measured. Once the measurements are taken in their local store, the information will be faxed to the store in your hometown, where the order will ultimately be filled. It's a great method and solves the problem of people showing up with different tux styles or lugging their tuxes on airplanes or trains. If you can't find such a service at one of your local tuxedo providers, ask your out-of-town ushers to go to a tailor in their hometown and be measured. It may cost a few dollars, but this is the only way to get accurate measurements.

**Our wedding will take place in the morning on a beach in Maui, Hawaii. I'm wearing a gown and I want my fiancé to wear something nice. What can he wear?**

Consider a **morning suit**, a light-colored men's suit. You can choose from white, cream, or gray.

**Should my fiancé rent his tuxedo or buy one?**

That depends. Do you and your fiancé go to formal events more than once a year? If so, owning a tuxedo is a plus. However, if this is the only chance he'll have to wear it, it's best to go with a rental.

# wedding rings

## Metal mania

$\mathcal{W}$edding rings symbolize your eternal bond. Most often, the bride and groom wear matching gold bands. When selecting rings, choose a metal that's durable enough to withstand day-to-day rigors. Traditionally, wedding rings are made of yellow gold, white gold, platinum, or a combination of these metals. (Platinum is twice as expensive as gold.) When it comes to gold, there are various levels of purity, and 14 karat and 18 karat are the most popular. (Be aware that 24 karat gold is actually too soft to be made into a durable wedding ring.)

To begin your ring search, look in magazines and visit jewelers. Try on different styles and see what looks best on both of you. Remember, as with wedding gowns, sometimes what you see in a catalog looks entirely different on your hand! And be sure to have you fiancé try on all of the matching styles as well—a flowery hand-engraved band could look great on you but too feminine on him. Or don't match your bands—choose entirely different styles that are the most complimentary for both of you.

# ASK THE EXPERTS

**How do we know if a ring we purchase is of high quality?**

When looking at wedding bands, check the inside of the ring. You should see two markings. One should tell you about the purity of the metal (i.e., 14k, 18k). The second is unique to the manufacturer and shows that they stand behind their merchandise.

**How much should we spend on our wedding bands?**

Plain platinum bands will set you back at least $400 each and can range as high as $650 per ring. If you opt for simple gold bands, expect to pay about $150 or $200 each. Designer rings—and those encrusted with diamonds or other gems—will cost significantly more. Engraving is usually included in these prices.

**We've heard friends talk about buying wedding bands online. Is this safe?**

Yes, it is. It's also very cost-effective because it eliminates the middle man—namely, the jewelry store. Here's how it works: You select a style you like from their Web site, and then the company, which is usually the manufacturer of the rings, mails you an order kit that includes ring shanks in a variety of widths along with a size guide. Once you determine your rings' widths and sizes, you can order a sample of the wedding band you've selected. Most online stores allow you to keep the ring for several days before you make a final decision. If you're happy with it, contact the company, place your order and return the sample ring in the preaddressed return envelope they will have provided. A leader in this market is Oromi (**www.oromi.com**, 201-868-1114).

# now what do I do?

## Answers to common questions

**Why do some bridal shops tear the manufacturer's label out of gowns?**

Unscrupulous bridal shops tear designer labels out of gowns so that brides-to-be can't determine the designer or style number. Basically, they do this so that future brides can't comparison-shop and call another store for a competitive price. This practice is illegal, but many bridal shops do it anyway. The rule of thumb: Don't shop at any store that won't tell you the manufacturer's name of the gown you're interested in.

**I'm a size 18, and I'm worried about finding a flattering wedding gown. I saw one gown that I fell in love with, but the designer doesn't make dresses in my size. Am I doomed?**

No, not at all! While it's true that not all designers make plus-size gowns, more of them are now creating gorgeous fashions for those of us who aren't a size 4. The following designers offer collections of larger-size gowns: Alfred Angelo, Bianchi, Bonny, Bridal Originals, Eden, Forever Yours, Jasmine, Jessica McClintock, Jim Hjelm, Mary's, Mon Cheri, Monique, Moonlight, Mori Lee, Private Label, Sweetheart, and Venus. If you still can't find the right gown, consider having a seamstress make one you love in your size.

**What should I do with my gown after the wedding?**

When you return from your honeymoon, have the gown professionally dry-cleaned, wrap it in cotton or muslin fabric and then store it flat—not on a hanger—in a cool, dry place. You can also consider using a gown-preservation service through a company like J. Scheer & Company (**www.jscheer.com**, 800-448-7291), WedClean (**www.wedclean.com**, 877-933-2532), Wedding Gown Preservation Company (**www.gownpreservation.com**, 800-305-3108) or Wedding Gown Specialists (**www.weddinggownspecialists.com**, 800-501-5005).

**I know that traditional wedding gowns are white, but that color makes me looked washed out. I'd rather wear a more flattering color!**

Your choice of wedding-gown color is totally up to you. Don't be a slave to tradition! Many designers have a wide selection of dresses in ivory, pale pink, pale blue, and even gold.

# OW WHERE DO I GO?!

## CONTACTS

Bridalgown.com

The Knot, **www.theknot.com**

For Tuxedos: International Formalwear Association, **www.formalwear.org**

## GOWN DESIGNERS

Alfred Angelo, **www.alfredangelo.com**

Bill Levkoff, **www.billlevkoff.com**

Champagne Formals, **www.champagneformals.com**

Daymor Couture, **www.daymor.com**

Dessy Creations, **www.dessy.com**

Galina, **www.galinabridals.com**

Jessica McClintock, **www.jessicamcclintock.com**

Jim Hjelm Occasions, **www.jimhjelmoccasions.com**

Jordan, **www.jordanfashions.com**

Nicole Miller, **www.nicolemiller.com**

Watters and Watters, **www.watters.com**

Vera Wang, **www.verawang.com**

## FLOWER GIRL DRESSES

Bridal Originals, **www.bridaloriginals.com**

Jessica McClintock, **www.jessicamcclintock.com**

Mary's, **www.marysbridal.com**

Mon Cheri, **www.mcbridals.com**

Sweetheart Gowns, **www.gowns.com**

## BOOKS

**Dresses for Your Wedding**
by Tracy Guth

**"I Do" Veils—So Can You! A Step-by-Step Guide to Making Bridal Headpieces, Hats and Veils With Professional Results**
by Claudia Lynch

**The Wedding Dress**
by Maria McBride-Mellinger

**Engagement & Wedding Rings, 2nd Edition: The Definitive Buying Guide for People in Love**
by Antoinette L. Matlins and Antonio C. Bonanno

CHAPTER

# 8

Whether you are having a religious service in a church or plan to make informal vows on
the beach, put some thought into the music, reading,  and rituals you select.
Whatever you choose should represent–and reinforce–
the promises you are making to each other.

# Ceremony Styles

# processionals and recessionals

## Who, where, and when

*T*he **processional** is the order in which your wedding party will enter the ceremony; the **recessional** is their order as they leave the ceremony. If you're getting married in a house of worship, your clergyman will explain any rules and offer suggestions. For an informal ceremony, after the ushers have escorted your guests to their seats, they should escort the bridesmaids down the aisle when the music starts, followed by the ring bearer and the flower girl. Lastly, of course, the bride is escorted down the aisle by her father, both parents, or whomever she chooses.

## Catholic Processional

- Priest, groom and best man walk down the aisle or approach from a side entrance and wait at the altar.
- Ushers paired with bridesmaids
- Maid of honor
- Ring bearer and flower girl
- The bride, escorted by her father, close family member, or friend

## Catholic Recessional

- Bride and groom (groom to the left of the bride)
- Ring bearer and flower girl
- Maid of honor and best man
- Bridesmaids and ushers (in pairs)
- Parents of the bride
- Parents of the groom

# ASK THE EXPERTS

**I am very self-conscious, and I hate the idea of being the center of attention while walking down that long aisle! Can't I just come in through a side door, close to the altar?**

If that's what you really want, talk with your officiant. This is your day, and you shouldn't do anything that makes you feel uncomfortable. That said, try and remember that this is about you and your beloved, whom you are meeting at the altar. The only eyes you should be concerned about are his.

## Jewish Processional

- Rabbi and cantor
- Grandparents of the bride
- Grandparents of the groom
- Ushers (in pairs, standing under the chuppah)
- Best man
- Groom, escorted by his parents (father on his right, mother on his left)
- Bridesmaids
- Maid of honor
- Ring bearer and flower girl
- Bride and her parents (father on her right, mother on her left)

## Jewish Recessional

- Bride and groom
- Bride's parents
- Groom's parents
- Bride's grandparents
- Groom's grandparents
- Ring bearer and flower girl
- Maid of honor and best man
- Bridesmaids and ushers (in pairs)
- Rabbi and cantor

# ceremony music

**Sweet melodies**

*W*hen choosing music for your ceremony, take time to listen to sample recordings and pick songs that mean something to you. If you marry in a house of worship, there may be specific rules about your music selections, so ask your clergyman before making any decisions.

Your instrumentation will depend on the ceremony's style and location and your own personal preferences. Popular choices include an organ, string trio, violinist, vocalist, guitarist, guitar/flute duo, and harp. Music from Broadway musicals, country music, and pop songs can also be appropriate, depending on the tone (and place) of your wedding.

---

## Traditional Ceremony Music

### PROCESSIONAL SELECTIONS

"Air" from Water Music Suite by George Frederic Handel

"Air on the G String" by Johann Sebastian Bach

"Bridal Chorus" ("Here Comes the Bride") by Richard Wagner

"Canon in D" by Johann Pachelbel

"Jesu, Joy of Man's Desiring" by Johann Sebastian Bach

"Wedding March" from The Marriage of Figaro
     by Wolfgang Amadeus Mozart

### RECESSIONAL SELECTIONS

"Allegro Maestoso" from Water Music Suite by George Frederic Handel

"Brandenburg Concerto No. 1" by Johann Sebastian Bach

"Fugue in E-Flat Major" from St. Anne by Johann Sebastian Bach

"Hallelujah Chorus" from The Messiah by George Frederic Handel

"Hornpipe" from Water Music Suite by George Frederic Handel

"Ode to Joy" by Ludwig von Beethoven

"Spring" from The Four Seasons by Antonio Vivaldi

"Wedding March" from A Mid-Summer's Night Dream
     by Felix Mendelssohn

---

# ASK THE EXPERTS

**We're on a tight budget but want the music at our church ceremony to be special.**

Chances are, your church works with an organist who will be happy to be the "musical director" of your event. Talk with him about your preferences. If you can't afford a professional vocalist, ask someone in the church choir if he or she is interested in taking part in your wedding. Another way to find musicians is to call a local music college. You may be able to find an existing string trio or singer who would be thrilled to sing at your event at a discounted rate. Don't forget to contact the American Federation of Musicians (**www.afm.org**, 212-869-1330), which can put you in contact with professional musicians in your area. But before you select anyone, be sure to hear them play!

**We have a list of ceremony music selections but we have no idea what to choose.**

When in doubt, ask the advice of the musicians you've hired. After all, they're professionals and perform at weddings all the time. Just make sure that you hear—and enjoy—a sample of the style of music they'll be playing at the wedding.

## Ceremony Programs

Many couples have a program printed so that their guests can follow along during the ceremony. This is especially helpful if your guests are not familiar with your religion or any wedding-specific traditions. A program is also a nice keepsake of your special day. It can contain a letter from the bride and groom, a story about how the couple met, the names of the wedding party and their relationships to the bride and groom, as well as a list of the music selections and readings. Some couples print programs on their own computer printers while others have them professionally printed along with their invitations. Your ushers will hand out the programs as your guests arrive.

# readings

**Underscore
shared values**

*T*he readings at your wedding will give you (and your guests) something to contemplate before the exchange of vows. These selections are meant to reinforce your religious beliefs as well as the meaning of love, loyalty, and marriage.

The readings usually take place after the opening prayer and remarks by the officiant. Someone in your bridal party can present a reading. Or you can ask a family member or friend to read—it's a lovely way to honor someone close to your heart who is not in the wedding party.

Depending on the rules of your church or synagogue, you can choose one or two readings from a holy text such as the Bible, the Book of Common Prayer, and the Torah. Poetry, literary works, and song lyrics may also be appropriate, depending on where your ceremony takes place. Remember, not all churches allow secular readings, so ask your officiant to clarify any stipulations beforehand.

Select your readings as far in advance as possible, and give your readers a photocopy. They will want to get acquainted with the text but should not feel compelled to memorize it.

Not all readings are taken from biblical or literary works. Here are two beautiful and heartfelt selections of Native American origin that you can incorporate into your ceremony:

## Blessing of the Apaches

Now you will feel no rain,
for each of you will be shelter for the other.
Now you will feel no cold,
for each of you will be warmth to the other.
Now there will be no loneliness,
for each of you will be companion to the other.
Now you are two persons,
but there is only one life before you.
May beauty surround you both in the journey ahead
and through all the years.
May happiness be your companion and your days together
be good and long upon the earth.

---

## Cherokee Prayer

God in heaven above please protect the ones we love.
We honor all you created as we pledge our hearts and lives together.
We honor Mother Earth and ask for our marriage to be abundant
and grow stronger through the seasons.
We honor Fire and ask that our union
be warm and glowing with love in our hearts.
We honor Wind and ask that we sail through life
safe and calm as in our father's arms.
We honor Water to clean and soothe our relationship
that it may never thirst for love.
With all the forces of the universe you created,
we pray for harmony and true happiness
as we forever grow young together.

# VOWS

**From this day forward…**

vow is a promise you make. If you're marrying in a church, certain elements will be standard. Talk with your officiant if there are any sections you are not 100 percent comfortable with—you may be able to tweak certain aspects. For informal ceremonies, you may write your own vows or at least customize them from preset selections.

If you do write your own vows, don't do it the night before the wedding! Your stress level will be high enough without the added pressure of having to be Robert Frost. Give yourselves plenty of time to work on your vows, several months ahead of time, and set a vow deadline of three weeks before the wedding. (If you can't do it, then skip it and find vows that have already been written.) Whatever you choose, make sure your vows are written clearly on a piece of paper or index card. To be safe on your wedding day, have your maid of honor carry your vows for you, while the groom-to-be can tuck his cards inside his suit pocket. While you may memorize your vows, there's no guarantee that you won't totally blank out as you gaze into your fiancé's eyes!

# Sample Vows

## CIVIL CEREMONY

I take you to be my lawfully wedded husband/wife. Before these witnesses, I vow to love you and care for you as long as we both shall live. I take you, with all your faults and your strengths, as I offer myself to you with my faults and my strengths. I will help you when you need help and will turn to you when I need help. I choose you as the person with whom I will spend my life.

## CATHOLIC VOWS

I take you to be my lawful husband/wife, to have and to hold from this day forward. I promise to be true to you in good times and in bad, in sickness and in health. I will love and honor you all the days of my life.

## EPISCOPAL VOWS

In the name of God, I take you to be my husband/wife, to have and to hold from this day forward, for better or worse, for richer or poorer, in sickness and health, to love and to cherish, until we are parted by death. This is my solemn vow.

# the rehearsal

Take it from
the top

*J*ust as a play needs a director, you need someone to coordinate the acts of your wedding ceremony and show the bridal party exactly what to do during the ceremony. This person can be your mom, maid of honor, trusted friend, officiant, or a hired wedding coordinator. Whomever you choose, don't pick yourself. This is the one time for the bride and groom to step back and relax.

During the rehearsal, your handpicked organizer will explain the order of the processional, teach the bridal party how to walk slowly and deliberately down the aisle, show the maid of honor how to tend to your train, and tell everyone how and where to stand during the ceremony. It's best to rehearse in the same space where the actual ceremony will be taking place.

If you have small children in your wedding party, remember that nothing will go according to your plan on the big day! Each child reacts differently under these circumstances. Some flower girls or ring bearers may become paralyzed with fear when they actually see the church filled with guests, some of whom they don't know. Others thrive on the excitement and do a splendid job. Just make a promise to yourself to accept whatever your young attendants choose to do—after all, they'll look adorable no matter what.

## FIRST PERSON　DISASTER STORY

### Flower Girl Fiasco

**W**hen we got married, we decided that my three-year-old niece should be our flower girl. She was fine at the rehearsal, but on the big day, she froze halfway down the aisle and wouldn't move—all these strange faces scared her. Her mother was my matron of honor and couldn't get to her. Fortunately, my grandmother held out a bag of candy, and my niece ran for it. It was a close call. I always tell my friends that if they plan to have little ones in their wedding party, it's best to stash some treats by the first pew.

**Christy P., Selma, Alabama**

# ASK THE EXPERTS

**Our officiant can't make it to the rehearsal. What should we do?**

While this sounds like distressing news, it's not as bad as you think. Remember, while this may be your first wedding, your officiant has presided over hundreds—maybe even thousands—of weddings. You should still schedule the rehearsal and have your wedding coordinator take charge of it. Once the members of your wedding party know what is expected of them, you'll feel more at ease. Also, make sure you go over the details with your officiant on the phone the day before the wedding. As long as there is an open line of communication, everything should be just fine.

**Can we hire an on-site wedding coordinator to organize only the rehearsal and the ceremony? That's all we need one for since we've planned everything else ourselves.**

It's an excellent idea to have someone in charge of the events at the ceremony. To find an on-site coordinator, ask your officiant for recommendations or contact the Association of Bridal Consultants (**www.bridalassn.com**, 860-355-0464).

# the rehearsal dinner

**Celebrating before the big day**

$\mathcal{T}$he day before your wedding is going to be so much fun—and so much work. You'll be tying up a million little loose ends and dealing with the emotions that are sure to come up when you are hours away from getting married. That's why you'll need a dinner celebration after the rehearsal—to kick back and relax! This is a time to reminisce with your family and friends and to share your dreams and hopes for the future in a more intimate setting than your reception will provide.

Generally, the groom's parents host this event. The guest list includes your immediate families and the entire wedding party, along with assorted spouses, significant others, out-of-town guests, and sometimes children. Many couples also invite their officiant and a guest.

The rehearsal celebration is typically held at a restaurant or at the home of the groom's parents and can be as formal or informal as you wish. Seating charts aren't necessary, but it's always nice to make sure the parents of the bride and groom are seated as close to the honored couple as possible.

# ASK THE EXPERTS

**We're hosting a destination wedding in the Bahamas. Our parents say we should invite all the guests to the rehearsal dinner, but shouldn't we limit it to the wedding party?**

Traditionally, only the immediate families of the bride and groom, the wedding party and their spouses or significant others are invited to the rehearsal dinner. In your case, if funds permit, a "welcome party" for all of your guests could work instead of a limited rehearsal dinner. Inquire about a beach clambake, a catamaran cruise, or other fun activities for you and your guests.

**Do we have to have a rehearsal dinner? We'd prefer to have a brunch or luncheon right after the rehearsal in the morning.**

Your rehearsal celebration can take place at any time—it does not have to be a dinner. In fact, if your rehearsal is in the morning, a brunch would be very convenient and probably more cost-effective than a dinner.

**We'd like to host a unique rehearsal dinner. Any ideas?**

Have you considered a theme rehearsal dinner? Try a Polynesian luau, a good old American barbecue, or a '50s evening complete with milkshakes, hamburgers, and fries. But don't get too elaborate—you don't want your rehearsal dinner to upstage your wedding.

**Are toasts or speeches given at rehearsal dinners?**

No, this is an informal evening. If it is a large gathering, it is customary for only the host to welcome the guests. To liven things up, you can have a projector set up to show slides of the bride and groom as children. Or go around the room and see if anyone has a funny or loving story to share about the bride or groom.

# now what do I do?

## Answers to common questions

**My fiancé and I met on a blind date at a rock concert. For our processional music, we'd like to have the musicians play a song by the band we saw that night. Is that possible?**

If you are marrying in a church, it may not be possible to stray from the preset list of music options. If that's the case, consider having your special song played for your first dance at the reception instead. But if circumstances allow, talk with your musicians ahead of time and ask them if they'll be able to arrange a rendition of the song so that it is appropriate for your ceremony. (You may have to provide them with sheet music or at least give them a recording to listen to.)

**We don't want to have the same ho-hum readings at our ceremony. Can we write a meaningful passage instead?**

That's a great idea! Your passage can be any length (although it's best if it's not too long) and written in any style. It can be a story about a significant turning point in your relationship, the love you've witnessed over the years while watching your parents' marriages, or a simple parable summing up the meaning of marriage.

**We're having a fairly small wedding with just a maid of honor and best man. Do we really need a rehearsal?**

It's always a good idea to have a rehearsal, if only to check that the ceremony site is in order. However, if everyone knows what's expected of them (and that includes where they will stand and how to exit) and you don't mind a misstep here or there, you can forego the rehearsal.

**My fiancé's parents are not hosting our rehearsal dinner, and we really can't afford to pay for one. Would it be rude to ask everyone for $20 to cover the restaurant bill?**

Yes. A better bet is to invite everyone over to your home for a potluck dinner or a simple spread of cheese and crackers, fruit and veggie platters, and a champagne toast. Remember, the idea behind the rehearsal dinner is simply for members of the wedding to get acquainted before the big day.

**My fiancé's best man is flying in the night before our wedding and can't make the rehearsal. How will he know what to do?**

First of all, hope for the best but prepare for the worst. Airline delays are the norm these days, and there's a chance he won't even make it to your wedding. Cross your fingers, but have your fiancé ask an usher to stand in for the best man at your rehearsal and explain to him that if the best man doesn't arrive, he's it! If the best man does arrive, your officiant and the stand-in usher will fill him in on the details.

**I would like both of my parents to walk me down the aisle. The problem is that they're divorced and neither wants the other involved.**

Talk with each parent privately and explain how you feel. Make them understand that it is very important to you that they both walk you down the aisle. Once the ceremony and photo taking are over, seat Mom and Dad at separate—but equally special—tables at the reception.

## NOW WHERE DO I GO?!

**CONTACTS**

The Ultimate Internet Wedding Guide
**www.ultimatewedding.com/vows**
This site has a wonderful collection of online vows.

**BOOKS**

**The Knot Guide to Wedding Vows and Traditions: Readings, Rituals, Music, Dances, Speeches and Toasts**
by Carley Roney

**Weddings From the Heart: Contemporary and Traditional Ceremonies for an Unforgettable Wedding**
by Daphne Rose Kingma

**African-American Wedding Readings**
by Tamara Nikuradse

**Sacred Threshold: Rituals and Readings for a Wedding With Spirit**
by Gertrud Mueller Nelson and Christopher Witt

**Wedding Readings: Centuries of Writing and Rituals on Love and Marriage**
by Eleanor C. Munro

**Alternative Weddings: An Essential Guide for Creating Your Own Ceremonies**
by Jane Ross-MacDonald

**The Everything Wedding Vows Book: Anything and Everything You Could Possibly Say at the Altar—And Then Some**
by Janet Anastasio and Michelle Bevilacqua

Your wedding day is finally here. All the decisions over music selections, seating charts, and how the napkins will be folded on the reception tables are finally behind you! The only thing that matters today is the joining of two people in matrimonial bliss. So take your time, survey the beauty of this occasion, and hold these memories in your heart forever.

# Your Wedding Day

# setting the mood

## Memories to last a lifetime

*G*et acquainted with butterflies now, because on the morning of your wedding, there are bound to be one or two flitting around in your stomach! That's only natural, but make yourself a promise: No matter what happens on the big day—if the flowers arrive wilted, the ring bearer gets ill, or the cake isn't exactly what you ordered—you won't freak out. In retrospect, these minor details won't matter (after all, you're the only one who will notice if the table linens are rose instead of blush pink).

This day is all about celebrating the fact that you and your fiancé found each other. If you catch yourself getting too nervous or annoyed because things aren't going exactly according to your plan, stop yourself. Take a deep, meditative breath and think about your soon-to-be husband. Relive in your mind the first time you and he met, the moment you knew it was love and the day he proposed. Concentrating on the really important things will calm you down and help you gain some perspective.

# ASK THE EXPERTS

**I want the morning of my wedding to be relaxing. I know I'll be fine, but how do I keep my parents from flipping out and making everyone crazy?**

Weddings can be very stressful, especially for the parents of the bride. For starters, try to tie up all the loose ends the day before the wedding so that the morning rush is more relaxed. Leave a nice, sentimental card for your parents to read over their morning coffee. In the note, explain how much you love them and appreciate everything they've done to make you happy. This will definitely put a smile on their faces. And if your parents do start to get nervous, tell them to take a deep breath and calm down. If you need to, assign a family member to be on "parent duty." This person can intervene if Mom and Dad start getting overly anxious.

## FIRST PERSON DISASTER STORY

### Attitude Is All

When we got married, the limo didn't show up, so I was late to the church. Our flower girl got nervous and walked down the aisle in tears. At our reception, a waiter dropped a tray of salads on my mother's gown and ruined it. I was a sobbing, nervous wreck! Looking back on it, I should have let those things roll off my back. Then I wouldn't have made my husband and family so uptight, and we all would have enjoyed the day. Instead, I foolishly let these stupid problems sour the mood—and our memories—of our wedding.

**Sarah T., Cambridge, Massachusetts**

# hair and makeup

## Dos and don'ts

*I*f you ask a professional beautician for advice concerning wedding-day makeup, the first thing he or she will say is this: Don't go for a whole new look. More good advice: Don't have a facial within two weeks of your wedding date. This is because a facial can actually cause an acne breakout—something you definitely want to avoid on your wedding day!

Next on the list of don'ts: Don't get a new haircut right before the wedding. You may end up hating it—along with how you look in all of your subsequent wedding photos. Instead, stick with a tried-and-true style (maybe incorporating a little something extra that's elegant and fancy), and have your stylist do a trial run to be sure that you'll like the end result.

Don't buy a different brand of makeup or try new colors on your wedding day. Again, stick with what you know and what looks best on you. If you do plan to purchase new makeup, make sure to have a consultation with a makeup artist at the counter or in a salon ahead of time. If you're having a professional beautician take care of makeup application on the day of your wedding, schedule a trial run several weeks before just in case you are allergic to her products.

Do be clear when explaining your expectations to your hairstylist and makeup artist. Better yet, provide them with photographs of similar hair and makeup styles to use as a guide. And remember the cardinal rule: Try it out *before* the big day.

# ASK THE EXPERTS

**I never wear makeup, and I don't want to wear any on my wedding day. My friends say I have to or I'll look washed out in the photos. Is this true?**

Yes. Remember, your photographer will be using high-powered flashes and professional camera equipment that captures everything—good and bad. If you aren't comfortable wearing makeup, at least carry some face powder with you. Apply this to your face to prevent oily spots from reflecting light in every photo. Make sure to apply powder to your forehead, chin, and nose.

**What's an updo?**

An **updo** is a style in which the hair is combed upward and piled atop the head. A tiara, crown, or simple bobby pins may be used to hold the hair in place. Make an appointment with your hairstylist to talk about the possibilities. If an updo isn't right for you, your stylist will suggest alternatives that will look just as lovely.

**A professional stylist is coming to help with my hair. How much time should I allot for this?**

Your time line will depend on your personality (are you low-maintenance or super-selective?) and how many people in the bridal party are having their hair done. If it's just you, set aside at least one hour. Most stylists that provide on-site services ask that your hair be clean and dry when they arrive so that they can begin styling immediately. Your stylist should be able to help you estimate how long she'll need for the other members of the bridal party.

# photography and videography

## Smile for the cameras

*T*his is the day when you truly are the star of the show. And since the photo opportunities can last all day and far into the night, make sure you're prepared—take along your makeup bag (or make sure that one of your bridesmaids gets it safely to the ceremony and reception).

Ideally, you should have three copies of the list of posed photographs you want to have taken. One copy is for you, one is for the photographer, and one is for whoever will be gathering your family and wedding party for the photographs. Because you don't need or want to have everyone standing around waiting to have their picture taken, have a designated person get the various groups together right before their photos. Most posed photo sessions take about half an hour to an hour, so keep some bottled water handy and your makeup bag nearby for touch-ups. Stay calm and relaxed and get used to showing those pearly whites!

Although you should have discussed it beforehand, it doesn't hurt to remind your photographer of any special shots you want taken. Have your wedding coordinator or maid of honor remind him throughout the day, and point out any close friends or family members who should be included in group photos.

# ASK THE EXPERTS

**I hired a videographer to ask guests at our reception to say a few words about us on tape, but my fiancé says that many of his friends will feel embarrassed and won't want to do it.**

Give the videographer specific instructions. He may approach each table, explain what he's doing and ask if anyone would like to participate. Tell your videographer to use his best judgment and to get as many people as he can on tape but not to persist with anyone who seems uncomfortable with the idea.

**My parents are bitterly divorced. They've both agreed to come to my wedding, and I would like to have some family pictures taken.**

Talk with your photographer and tell him about the situation— nothing could be worse than for him to try to pose your parents as if they were still a happily married couple. Once your photographer knows the situation, he will arrange the group shots with this in mind, making sure Mom and Dad are not right next to each other. Next, prepare each parent individually by explaining that you'd like some family photos, so they'll need to put aside their differences for your wedding day.

# the ceremony

Gulp—it's really
happening

*B*efore you leave for the ceremony, grab your emergency kit. This bag should contain an extra pair of pantyhose, your make-up, a brush, tissues, aspirin, antacids, a pair of comfortable shoes, and the phone numbers of all of your wedding vendors.

When entering the limousine, tread carefully. Enter the car last, and stand sideways, facing the front of the limo. Lift your skirt and any underskirts to knee height and lift your leg into the limo while setting your bottom firmly on the seat. Then gently slide the rest of your body into place.

Before the ceremony, make sure your wedding coordinator, mother, or best friend is on duty to oversee details such as program placement and proper guest seating. At a church ceremony, it's traditional to have ushers seat the bride's family and guests on the left side and the groom's family and friends on the right. (The sides are reversed for those marrying in a synagogue.)

When you arrive at the church, the person you've selected to walk you down the aisle should be standing there to whisk you into a "ready" room and keep you tucked safely out of sight.

# ASK THE EXPERTS

**A one-way limousine will bring us to the wedding site, and I've arranged for a minivan to pick up the bridal party after the reception. What and when should I tip the limo and minivan drivers?**

Drivers should be tipped 15 to 20 percent of the total fare at the last departure point. For your limo driver, tip when you get to the reception site. However, it's best to give this task to the best man or maid of honor, since you may forget a small detail like this in all the excitement.

**Our minister has told us on multiple occasions that if we don't arrive at the church on time, our ceremony will be cut short. Is this really possible?**

This may very well be true. Remember, churches often schedule many different events on the same day. Another wedding, baptism, or service may be taking place shortly after your ceremony. It's always best to adhere to the agreed-upon schedule, lest you run the risk of an abbreviated ceremony.

**I cry easily, and I'm pretty sure I'm going to cry during my wedding. I'm worried I'm going to wreck my makeup and gown. What should I do?**

Tears of joy are natural, especially on your wedding day. Just be sure to have a handkerchief handy to dab your eyes with.

# the reception

**Eat, drink, and be married**

*Y*our married friends have probably already warned you that many brides and grooms never eat a morsel of food at their wedding reception. The problem stems from things like an overly long receiving line and posed photo sessions that cut into the cocktail hour and dinner. There is a lot to digest (pardon the pun) during your reception. If you wish to enjoy your meal, remember these simple tips:

- Tell your photographer to get as many of the posed shots before and directly after the ceremony so that you and the bridal party can enjoy the cocktail hour and dinner.

- Ask your photographer to make the rounds during dinner and to take a group picture of each table.

- If you've already greeted your guests in the receiving line (see below), curb the temptation to start your table-to-table rounds during dinner. Instead, have a little something to eat and visit the tables during the serving of the cake.

- If you are still being pulled in every direction, tell the wait staff for your table to keep a plate warm for the two of you to nibble on later.

# ASK THE EXPERTS

**Our reception will take place in a local hall, which we can decorate the morning of the wedding. Should I do this or should I ask a friend to handle it?**

Definitely ask a friend or family member, or hire a wedding decorator or designer to take care of this task. Your wedding day will be incredibly hectic without having to do this, too. If you are a micromanager, feel free to visit the site while others are decorating. Put in your two cents and then get back to preparing for the ceremony.

**We'd like to give the reception centerpieces away at the end of the evening. What's the best way to do this?**

That's a lovely gesture, especially when you consider that a centerpiece can cost anywhere from $50 to $200. (Moreover, some reception-room decorators charge a fee to remove them to another location.) You can have the D.J. or M.C. announce that the bride and groom wish to give their guests the centerpieces as a memento of the event and that the person with the birthday closest to the wedding date gets the centerpiece.

**We'd like to have a garter belt toss and flower toss. When are they done?**

Both are done toward the end of the reception. For the garter belt toss, the bride needs to sit on a chair in the middle of the room and let her new husband slip the garter off her leg. He then throws it to a waiting group of single men. Whoever catches the garter is supposedly the next to marry. After the garter toss comes the bouquet toss. (These days, brides often have their florist create a second "toss" bouquet so that they don't have to give up their flowers.) The woman who catches the bouquet is then supposed to sit in the chair while the man who caught the garter slips it on her leg. Or you can simply ask the "catchers" to dance with each other instead.

## The Receiving Line

A receiving line, in which the entire bridal party greets each guest, is expected at most weddings since it will be the first—and possibly the only—opportunity your guests will have to personally congratulate you. The line begins with your maid of honor, best man, bridesmaids and ushers, followed by your parents, and you and your new husband. If you're having a very large wedding, you may wish to drop this ritual in favor of visiting each table during the dinner service. It's very important that at some point during the wedding, either the bride or groom personally greet each guest.

# wedding toasts

## Champagne wishes

A wedding reception would not be complete without a few **toasts**—a ritual in which brave souls say a few kind words about the bride and groom, often including funny childhood anecdotes. The first toast is traditionally given by the best man. After the best man, the groom usually says a few words of thanks. He is followed by the bride (if she wishes), then her parents or closest family member, ending finally with the groom's parents or closest family member. These days, tradition is open to interpretation, so feel free to ask anyone in your party to speak. Whether it's a traditional or nontraditional reception, one rule holds true: No toast should last longer than four minutes.

It's a good idea to introduce each toaster before they speak. You can have your band leader or D.J. do this, or for a more personal touch, ask someone from your wedding party to act as M.C. It's also a very good idea to have a handheld microphone available so that everyone can hear what's being said. A small podium is nice too, especially if the toastmasters will be using note cards—which is not a bad idea.

# cutting the cake

**The classic photo op**

The wedding cake is symbolic of your celebration—it's a sumptuous dessert meant exclusively for this occasion. The cutting of the cake is one of the most anticipated events at any wedding. Tons of photos will be snapped during this mini ceremony. You'll hold the knife together and cut a slice of cake. (Don't worry, most often one slice is already precut, and all you'll have to do is follow the advice of your coordinator or banquet manager.) Remove the piece of cake and then feed a bite to each other, while smiling for the cameras.

Most couples wish to reserve the top layer or a piece of the cake to take home and freeze. On your first anniversary, you're supposed to defrost the cake and eat it. Though this is a sentimental tradition, it's not a good idea as the cake will be inedible.

# parting gifts

**Saying thank you**

You'll receive a lot of gifts on your wedding day, but you should also consider giving a few. Before the ceremony, give your parents thoughtful cards with handwritten notes inside. Special engraved photo frames are another nice touch for both sets of parents and grandparents, in anticipation of the wedding photos to come.

The bridal party should also receive a little something special to mark the occasion. Jewelry to match the bridesmaids' gowns is always a popular choice. A photo frame, spa-treatment gift certificate, snow globe, music box, or book of poetry are other great options. For your ushers, watches, Swiss Army knives, and cufflink sets are nice mementos. (The groom is in charge of getting the ushers' gifts.)

The bride and groom also often exchange gifts on the wedding day. Engraved toasting glasses, wedding journals to record your memories of the day, crystal photo frames, or items for your new home may be ideal.

## Fabulous Favors

While you are not obligated to provide guests with a **favor** (a small parting gift), it's a wonderful way to say thank you to everyone who took part in your special day. Favors can be simple (homemade chocolates) or elaborate (custom-designed jewelry boxes). Here are a few ideas:

- A bag of homemade cookies tied with ribbon and a recipe card

- Chocolate roses tied with a ribbon

- A packet of flower seeds with your names and wedding date printed on the front

- A small grapevine wreath decorated with silk flowers

- A "glass" slipper filled with confetti (or sugar-coated Jordon almonds)

- A miniature snow globe

- A book of poetry with a handwritten thank-you from the bride and groom on the inside front cover

# tying up loose ends

### Living happily
### ever after

$\mathcal{S}$ome couples prefer to change into casual clothes at the end of the ceremony and slip out the back door while others prefer to make a more grand exit—in a helicopter, for instance. Still others decide to make their special occasion last even longer, and they invite everyone to a goodbye breakfast or brunch the following morning. What you choose to do depends on the location and style of your wedding. Those who prefer to say goodbye with panache can opt for something as simple as a limousine or as elaborate as a horse-drawn carriage.

If you decide to sneak away, make sure at least to say goodbye and thank you to your immediate family and bridal party. If you are hosting a breakfast or brunch the next day, be sure that everyone has the details—when and where—before you leave the reception. You won't want any interruptions on your wedding night, so put someone else in charge and have your guests call them with any questions.

# ASK THE EXPERTS

**We don't plan on staying until the very end of our reception since we'd prefer to spend some quiet time at home before leaving for our Caribbean honeymoon. Can we do this, or will our vendors need to speak with us at the end of the night?**

Most often, all of your wedding services will be prepaid, so your vendors shouldn't have to speak with you about anything. However, make sure you put someone else in charge of handing out any tips in your absence (such as to the lead singer in the band or the wedding party's limo drivers). The best man or father of the bride usually handles this. Also, leave instructions for the cleanup crew. Do you want any of the leftover favors or wedding programs? Should any extra food be donated to a local homeless shelter? Should the floral centerpieces be sent to a local retirement home?

**We are holding our reception at a hometown hotel, which has provided us with a suite for our wedding night. We're tempted to invite our friends to our room for a late-night party after the reception.**

Carefully consider this before making a decision. You may want some privacy directly after the wedding, or you may be pooped and just want to go right to sleep! However, if you rarely see out-of-town friends and family members, you may prefer to spend some time with them. Sharing your most happy occasion with everyone is very generous. Just make sure that you schedule enough quiet time for the two of you after all the craziness.

**Due to sudden work obligations, we have to postpone our honeymoon for a few weeks after our wedding. Going home after our reception seems so unromantic. What should we do?**

You're right to be concerned. Regardless of whether you are eloping or have to postpone your honeymoon, spend your first married night at a nice hotel, ideally one that is close to your reception site.

# now what do I do?

## Answers to common questions

**I am so nervous about my wedding day. What if everything goes wrong?**

First of all, take a long, deep breath. Now exhale. Repeat this phrase to yourself: "Everything is going to be all right. Everything is going to be all right." Whatever happens on your wedding day, let it roll right off your back. Hopefully, it will all be perfect, but if minor mishaps occur, don't get too upset. The important thing is that you have found the love of your life and you are celebrating a happy occasion with your loved ones. Does it really matter if the sun isn't shining or the cake isn't chocolate?

**My parents passed away a long time ago, but I would like to include their memory in our day. May I read a letter to them at the reception?**

Everyone will be touched by your sentiments, and your letter will no doubt bring back fond memories of your parents for many of your guests. This will probably be a tough letter to get through, so have your new husband stand by your side for support—and don't be embarrassed to take a tissue break here or there.

**My fiancé and I put together a videotape consisting of clips from our childhoods. We'd like to have it played at our reception.**

Ask your reception-site manager or wedding coordinator to take care of this for you. There may be an extra charge for the rental of a VCR and video screen, but it will be worth it. You and your guests will enjoy taking a stroll down memory lane while celebrating your bright future as a couple.

**We have chosen a buffet for our reception meal. Our banquet-hall manager told us that there are usually leftovers. What should we do with them?**

While you may ask for the leftovers to be boxed up, for safety reasons, some reception locations prohibit food from being taken home. Other sites suggest that the food be brought to a local homeless shelter or food bank. Talk it over with your fiancé and/or wedding coordinator and decide ahead of time what you'd like to do with the leftovers. If you are donating them to a shelter, contact them beforehand to iron out the delivery details.

**I am not good with sappy, emotional moments. I'd like to write everyone in my bridal party a note of thanks to include with their presents, but I don't want them reading the notes while we're around. Any suggestions?**

Have your gift and letter delivered to each member of the bridal party the day after your wedding. They will still be on a high from your event, but you won't be overwhelmed by emotional friends and family.

**We're inviting a few old fraternity friends of my fiancé's to our wedding. I'm worried that the drinking will get out of hand at our reception. What can I do?**

Wedding bartenders generally don't cut off your guests, so ask a few of your fiancé's ushers to watch for any signs of trouble. You can also request that liquor stop being served at a specific time during the reception.

## OW WHERE DO I GO?!

**CONTACTS**

TheKnot.com

ModernBride.com

WeddingChannel.com

**BOOKS**

The Portable Wedding Consultant: Invaluable Advice From the Industry's Experts for Saving Your Time, Money and Sanity
by Leah Ingram

What No One Tells the Bride: Surviving the Wedding, Sex After the Honeymoon, Second Thoughts, Wedding Cake Freezer Burn and Becoming Your Mother
by Marg Stark

The Everything Wedding Organizer: Checklists, Calendars and Worksheets for Planning the Perfect Wedding
by Laura Morin

After the vows have been spoken, the cake has been cut, and your guests have gone home, it's time to revel in your new life together. Plan ahead to make your honeymoon a special getaway, whether it's a low-key weekend at a nearby bed-and-breakfast or a month-long trek through the Himalayas.

# The Honeymoon

# wedding decompression

## It's transitional time

### Ideal Time to Travel

**ORLANDO**
October through May

**LAS VEGAS**
October through April

**HAWAII**
Ideal all year

**\*ISLANDS**
All year

**\*BERMUDA**
May through September

**\*JAMAICA/ARUBA**
All year

**PARIS/LONDON/VENICE**
April through October

**BALI/AUSTRALIA**
All year, especially December through March when it's summer there

*Hurricane season is June through October. Getting traveler's insurance is wise (see page 177).

The wedding is over, and now it's time for just the two of you to celebrate. It's also time to decompress and relax following a hectic few months of furious wedding planning. It's natural to feel a bit let down after the anticipation leading up to the big day and the excitement of the actual event. And it's normal to be nervous, too: After all, now you'll start referring to your former boyfriend, beloved, and fiancé as "my husband."

That's why it's very important to spend some of your wedding preparation time thinking about what will happen after the wedding. Plan your honeymoon as carefully as you've planned your big day. Whether you decide to take a long vacation in the outback or to spend just a night away at a local beachfront hotel, your honeymoon will be a special time for you both to remember throughout all of your married life.

Your honeymoon will also be a time of transition into being a married couple. Try to ease into it—just relax and remember to have a good time. The wedding chaos is finally behind you.

## Something To Think About...

■ Do pack at least one week before your trip. Packing the day of your wedding is too stressful. Also, be sure to pack a carry-on bag containing medical supplies, passports (if needed), and one change of clothes for each of you—just in case your luggage gets lost.

■ Do confirm flights the day before you leave. And leave an emergency number where you can be reached.

■ Don't plan too many activities for the day after your wedding. Chances are you'll both be too tired.

■ Don't bring the thank-you stationery along. Write your notes when you get back.

■ Do plan to spend at least one night away at a hotel if you can't get away for a honeymoon. You need a place to transition from singlehood to married life.

■ Do try to spend part of your honeymoon alone together. Remember that this is your first chance to celebrate as a married couple in an intimate way.

## FIRST PERSON DISASTER STORY

### The Exhausted Bride

Sam and I had a huge wedding with 250 guests. We had a wonderful time, but we should have treated our honeymoon more as a place to unwind than as a regular vacation. We had an exhausting plane ride right after the reception, followed by a five-city sightseeing trip. We were already running around to museums when I realized that what I really wanted to do was get some rest, lie on a beach, and cuddle with my new husband! I wish we had saved our grand European vacation for an anniversary trip and had had a more relaxing and intimate honeymoon instead.

**Julia T., Brooklyn, New York**

# honeymoon styles

**Something for everyone**

*T*here are many honeymoon styles, so before you make any definitive plans, explore them all. For those with a larger budget, consider pampering yourself. Try a cruise, an all-inclusive package at a resort (similar to a cruise, with lodging, food, and activities all included in the price) or a fancy hotel with a wide range of amenities. These vacations tend to be a bit upscale and require some dressy attire for more formal evenings out.

Active honeymoons—in which you and new spouse spend time hiking, fishing, boating, etc.—are becoming more popular. It can mean white-water rafting down the Colorado River, camping in Antigua, or biking through Vermont.

For some, relaxation goes hand in hand with getting back to nature. Country honeymoons at smaller lodgings, such as a bed-and-breakfast or a quaint inn, are a real treat since innkeepers can personalize your stay with amenities such as flowers and champagne upon your arrival, breakfast in bed, or a picnic basket for an afternoon out by the lake.

Money is often tight after a wedding, and you may be tempted to forego the honeymoon right away. Don't! Instead, consider taking a short, inexpensive honeymoon. You owe it to yourselves to take a break after the wedding. It doesn't matter where you go or how much you spend—all that matters is that you're together.

# ASK THE EXPERTS

**I love nature, and I'd like to hike and swim on our honeymoon. The problem is, my fiancé isn't much of an outdoorsman.**

Research vacation spots that offer outdoor activities in the vicinity of larger hotels or resorts. One possibility is the Caribbean island of St. Lucia, where you can enjoy full-service accommodations in close proximity to activities such as hiking and water sports. For something on the mainland, consider Stowe, Vermont. In the winter, it's a skiers' haven, while the summer transforms the area into a backpacker's paradise with a variety of gorgeous inns and bed-and-breakfasts.

**We went to a travel agent to book a low-cost honeymoon, but the cheapest packages were between $599 and $699 per person!**

A honeymoon doesn't have to break the bank. (That said, the average price of a nine-day honeymoon is about $3,500.) A major expense of any honeymoon is airfare. If you pick somewhere within driving distance, you can avoid that outlay of cash. The next step is to find accommodations that you'll enjoy while not cleaning out your pockets. Ask about weekend or weekday specials, honeymoon packages and auto-club rates. You can also select a location that offers a kitchenette so that you can fix some meals in your room. Or you can splurge on one night in a fancy bed-and-breakfast or hotel rather than taking a longer vacation.

# booking the honeymoon

## Package or à la carte?

$\mathcal{S}$ome couples choose to entrust the task of arranging this getaway of a lifetime to a professional and use a full-service travel agent. If you go this route, make sure you hire an experienced agent who spcializes in honeymoon and romance travel. He or she should be familiar with a multitude of honeymoon destinations—at every budget level—and have some firsthand comments about your choices. To find a qualified travel agent, contact the American Society of Travel Agents (**www.astanet.com**, 703-739-2782). Request a list of agents who specialize in honeymoons.

When first approaching an agent, have some ideas about the type of trip you want to take. Let the agent know your budget, how many days and nights you wish to be away and what type of lodging (resort, hotel, bed-and-breakfast, inn, motel) you prefer. Your agent will ask you if you're interested in room-only, a package, or all-inclusive. **Room-only** is exactly what it sounds like: You are booking your lodging and purchasing everything else separately. A **package** can include round-trip airfare and transfers, hotel accommodations, a few meals, and discounts on local attractions. **All-inclusive** means that your hotel, meals, drinks, taxes, and gratuities are included in one predetermined price.

While all-inclusives and packages may sound tempting, make sure you'll utilize what's included. Remember, when booking an all-inclusive, you've prepaid for all meals. If you end up not enjoying the food at the resort, you're out of luck because you've already paid for it.

# ASK THE EXPERTS

**We are interested in honeymooning at an all-inclusive resort in Jamaica, but there are so many to choose from!**

Ask everyone you know for recommendations. Then hit the Internet and search various newsgroups that cover Caribbean travel by going to **http://groups.google.com**. Type in resorts you're considering, and you should find comments from other travelers. Other travel portals such as **Fodors.com** and **Frommers.com** also offer reviews of accommodations around the world. And don't forget to ask your travel agent. However, remember to take his comments with a grain of salt. Some resorts offer special incentives to agents, so you may feel him pushing you toward one venue over another.

**We want to book a package tour to Italy for our honeymoon, which we'll have to prepay. What happens if we cancel or postpone the trip?**

That depends on the tour operator and the package. Before signing on the dotted line, read the fine print carefully. Most packages do have cancellation and refund policies.

**What about traveler's insurance?**

If your package doesn't have a refund policy for emergency cancellations and you're spending a lot of money, then get traveler's insurance. For $35 to $75, you can get insurance to cover everything from trip cancellation to trip interruption, not to mention lost baggage. Most travel agencies sell travel insurance.

# Orlando

**More than
just the Mouse**

*O*rlando is one of the most popular domestic destinations for honeymooners. With an average yearly daytime temperature of about 73 degrees, theme parks galore, and tons of outdoor activities including world-class golf, tennis, and swimming, it's a no-brainer. Orlando means great weather and a never-ending to-do list.

The area also offers accommodations in every budget range. The only downside for honeymooners can be the children quotient—after all, Orlando is home to such delights as Walt Disney World, Sea World, and Universal Studios, all favorite choices for family vacations. But if you don't mind rubbing elbows with the younger set, you'll do just fine. Start by contacting the Orlando/Orange County Convention & Visitors Bureau (**www.orlandoinfo.com**, 800-646-2087) and request a free Orlando vacation planning kit and the Orlando Magicard, which offers discounts on lodging, meals, attractions, and more.

## Orlando Area Attractions

Busch Gardens Tampa Bay
& Adventure Island Tampa
(**www.buschgardens.com**, 800-372-1797)

Cypress Gardens
(**www.cypressgardens.com**, 800-282-2123)

Daytona International Speedway
(386-947-6404)

Discovery Cove Orlando
(**www.discoverycove.com**, 877-434-7268)

Kennedy Space Center
(321-449-4400)

Sea World Orlando
(**www.seaworld.com**, 800-327-2424)

Richard Petty Driving Experience
(**www.1800bepetty.com**, 800-237-3889)

Universal Studios and Islands of Adventure
(**www.universalstudios.com**, 877-837-2273)

Walt Disney World
(**www.disney.com**, 407-934-7639)

# ASK THE EXPERTS

### Where's the beach?

Orlando is located in the middle of the state, so you'll have to drive about an hour and a half to get to a beach. But the beaches are beautiful. Head for Daytona Beach, New Smyrna Beach, or Cocoa Beach (near the Kennedy Space Center).

### We want to visit theme parks, but we'd like to stay in an upscale resort.

A beautiful hotel to consider is the Peabody Orlando (**www.peabody-orlando.com**, 800-PEABODY). Just 15 minutes from Orlando International Airport, the Peabody offers special services that are ideal for newlyweds. They'll arrange for breakfast in bed, secure tee times for a round of golf, get you a table at a hot dining spot, and more. The hotel also offers a pool, spa facilities, an outdoor whirlpool, and tennis.

Other upscale accommodations in the Orlando area include the Hyatt Regency Grand Cypress (**www.hyattgrandcypress.com**, 800-554-9288), Disney's Yacht & Beach Club Resort (**www.disneyworld.com**, 407-W-DISNEY), and Portofino Bay Hotel at Universal Studios Escape (**www.universalstudios.com**, 877-837-2273).

### Where can we catch live music in Orlando?

Citywalk at Universal Studios Orlando (**www.universalstudios.com**, 877-837-2273) is a great place to eat, drink, and dance. If you're staying on Disney property, don't miss Downtown Disney Pleasure Island (**www.disney.com**, 407-934-7781). Besides a multitude of dance clubs, you'll find the House of Blues for a meal and live entertainment, DisneyQuest for the ultra-arcade and virtual-reality experience and Cirque du Soleil performances.

# Las Vegas

## Romance on the Strip

$\mathscr{V}$iva Las Vegas! There are some gorgeous new hotels in this city, in addition to dozens of old standbys. The allure of Vegas is, of course, the casinos, but you can have lots of fun and play down the gambling, if you wish. Vegas is a shopper's paradise, with countless malls, specialty shops, and boutiques. Many of the hotels offer exquisite amenities, including health clubs, spas, pool/recreation areas, and more. And if you're a food lover, there are many jewels to be discovered, including Bally's famous Sterling Sunday Brunch, Emeril Lagasse's New Orleans Fish House, and Wolfgang Puck's Spago.

Many couples visit Las Vegas purely for the shows and other entertainment. Only in this city can you peruse the outstanding art exhibitions at Bellagio and see a volcano erupt at The Mirage, visit leopards and bottlenose dolphins at The Secret Garden of Siegfried & Roy, and take an elevator ride to the top of the Eiffel Tower at Paris Las Vegas—all before the sun sets!

Start your honeymoon planning by visiting the official Web site of the Las Vegas Convention and Visitors Authority or simply by calling (**www.lasvegas24hours.com**, 800-332-5333).

The Luxor Hotel and Casino in Las Vegas

# ASK THE EXPERTS

### Which part of town should we stay in?

Las Vegas is composed of two areas: the Strip and Downtown. As you land at McCarran International Airport, you'll see the Strip, a three-and-a-half mile length of road that connects many major hotels and casinos. The other side of the coin is Downtown, which was developed first and is still home to some of the older casinos. In recent years, new developments have revitalized this area. If you're looking for glitz and easy access to many casinos, your best bet is to stay in the Strip. If you prefer something a bit more relaxed (if you can call any part of Las Vegas relaxed!), then Downtown may be appropriate. The best thing you can do is to search the Internet for casino/hotel sites and determine which area looks best for you.

### What's the weather like?

From May through September, it's hot, hot, hot, with average temperatures ranging from 88 to 105 degrees! Protect yourselves by drinking plenty of water throughout the day to avoid dehydration and by wearing a sunblock of at least SPF 30 whenever you're out-doors. The rest of the year daytime temperatures can fluctuate between 56 and 81 degrees.

### We'd like to indulge in a spa treatment while in Las Vegas.

Most of the major hotel/casinos have spa facilities. Here are some top spots: Bellagio Spa (**www.bellagio.com**, 702-693-7472), The JW Marriott Las Vegas (**www.gowestmarriott.com/lasvegas**, 877-869-8777), Canyon Ranch Spa Club at The Venetian (**www.venetian.com**, 888-283-6423), Four Seasons Spa (**www.fourseasons.com/lasvegas**, 877-632-5000), and Spa Mandalay at Mandalay Bay Resort (**www.mandalaybay.com**, 877-632-7000).

# Hawaii

Aloha!

Hawaii is a glorious collection of six volcanic islands: Oahu, Maui, Kauai, Lanai, Molokai, and the Big Island called Hawaii. The weather is always great—about 60 degrees in winter and 85 degrees in summer. If you like lounging in the sun, Hawaii is for you since almost every day is a beach day. Each island has its own individual charms, so plan on visiting more than one.

You've no doubt heard of Honolulu and Waikiki Beach. Oahu is home to both of these famous destinations. Its pace is much more active than that of Kauai or Maui. Oahu is pure natural beauty, with the addition of man-made attractions such as museums, art galleries, nightclubs, and five-star restaurants. If Oahu is your home base during your honeymoon, you'll be able to visit Pearl Harbor and the Arizona Memorial.

Maui is a favored spot for honeymooners. With 42 miles of beachfront, it will be relatively easy to pick a resort with an ocean view. On Maui, you can hike a dormant volcano, golf, lie on the beach, enjoy a gourmet meal, or go on a whale-watching expedition.

Growing in popularity is Kauai—also known as the Garden Island—for its forests, beaches, and Waimea Canyon (the Grand Canyon of the Pacific). Enjoy windsurfing, whale watching, helicopter tours, and horseback riding along stretches of pristine beach.

Fewer than 3,000 people live on Lanai, the "Pineapple Island." It was given this nickname because for more than 70 years 16,000 acres of it was a pineapple plantation run by Dole Foods Company. Today, there are two very elegant hotels located there: the Lodge at Koele and the Manele Bay Hotel, both of which offer terrific golf courses. The island is friendly, although a bit off the beaten path. But you'll find plenty to keep you busy, including diving, horseback riding, mountain biking, sailing, fishing, and tennis.

Molokai is the least developed of the Hawaiian islands, but you'll drink in the South Seas lifestyle while relaxing on the "Friendly Isle." Here, you'll meet your share of authentic fishermen and seafarers.

On the Big Island of Hawaii, you can visit the Hawaii Volcanoes National Park and learn about how this island chain was created. In fact, some islands, like the Big Island, are still growing, as lava from its volcanoes continues to pour into the Pacific. Activities on this island include golfing, horseback riding, and even snow skiing.

 **ASK THE EXPERTS**

**How can we learn more about Hawaiian honeymoons?**

Start your research at **www.gohawaii.com**, the official Web site of the Hawaii Visitors & Convention Bureau. Request a free vacation planner, and learn about the six Hawaiian islands. Also contact Pleasant Holidays (**www.pleasantholidays.com**, 800-7HAWAII), a very reputable firm specializing in vacations to Hawaii, Tahiti, and Mexico. Many airlines also offer package trips to the islands.

# cruising

## The open sea

*E*ven if you've never been on a cruise, you may wish to consider one for your honeymoon. First of all, there has been intense competition among cruise lines scrambling to build the biggest and best cruise ships in the world. The outcome is a hefty inventory of empty staterooms that are not being booked at full price. This means that snagging a cruise at a discount is relatively easy, especially if you book through a cruise specialist.

The more appealing aspect of cruising, however, is that it is all-inclusive. For one package price, you get airfare (although you can book air travel separately), a stateroom, all meals, and entertainment. Your only other expenses will be alcohol, shore excursions (which are optional), souvenirs, and tips. And there is now "one-class" service on all ships, which means that booking any cabin, no matter where it's located, entitles you to the same service, meals, and other perks as everyone else onboard.

Cruise lines offer voyages as short as three days and as long as three months. Destinations are as numerous as there are ports of call. Popular itineraries include the Caribbean islands, Mexico, Hawaii, Alaska, and Bermuda.

Each ship is also different—some are floating resorts with massive capacity while others are more intimate. Carefully research different lines to determine which cruise style is best for you.

# ASK THE EXPERTS

**How do we find a travel agent who specializes in cruises?**

Ask if your agent is affiliated with the Cruise Lines International Association (**www.cruising.org**, 212-921-0066). Certified cruise counselors have taken courses in selling cruise packages and have sailed on or personally inspected many of the ships.

**We have booked a cruise from Miami to the Caribbean islands. Do we need passports?**

Check with your travel agent or the cruise line directly just to be safe. Some islands, such as Puerto Rico and the U.S. Virgin Islands, do not require passports for American citizens. However, other islands do require this documentation if you are planning on going ashore.

**What if we get seasick?**

Cruise lines do their best to route ships through calm waters during most of the year, but the occasional storm can pose a problem. However, many of the ships have adopted special stabilizers to soften the blows during harsh weather. That said, it's not a bad idea to plan for the worst and bring some over-the-counter medications to alleviate motion sickness.

**We've heard that dinner seating on cruise ships is communal, but what if we want intimate meals?**

When booking your trip, make sure to get details on table-for-two dining. On some ships, you'll find that this luxury is first-come, first-served, or you may need to book a certain room category to enjoy this perk. A few cruise lines that offer tables for two are: Celebrity Cruises (**www.celebritycruises.com**), Costa Cruise Lines (**www.costacruises.com**), Cunard Line (**www.cunardline.com**), Holland America (**www.hollandamerica.com**), Norwegian Cruise Line (**www.ncl.com**), Princess Cruises (**www.princesscruises.com**), Radisson Seven Seas Cruises (**www.rssc.com**), Seabourn Cruise Line (**www.seabourn.com**), and Windstar Cruises (**www.windstarcruises.com**).

# fun in the sun

**Puerto Rico, the U.S. Virgin Islands, and the Bahamas**

There are many fantastic Caribbean honeymoon locations, but this trio—Puerto Rico, the U.S. Virgin Islands, and the Bahamas—offers something special for newlyweds.

Puerto Rico has it all: beaches, a tropical rain forest, nightlife, a fascinating culture steeped in 500 years of history, and eclectic restaurants and casinos. And since it's the easternmost island of the Greater Antilles (two-and-a-half hours southeast of Miami), it's a hub for connecting flights to many other Caribbean islands. To learn more, contact the Puerto Rico Tourism Company (**www.prtourism.com**, 800-223-6530).

For those drawn to the sea, the U.S. Virgin Islands in the Lesser Antilles—St. Thomas, St. John's and St. Croix—are an ideal getaway. You can enjoy diving, snorkeling, sailing, fishing, swimming, duty-free shopping, and more. Each island has its own special qualities, but all three boast hotels and resorts fit for royalty. The weather is unbeatable, with high 70s in winter and low 80s in summer. For more information, contact the U.S.V.I. Department of Tourism (**www.usvi.org**, 800-372-USVI).

Ah, the Bahamas! You've got your work cut out for you when choosing this spot, since it's actually made up of many islands, including Grand Bahama, the Bimini Islands, Nassau/Paradise Island, Andros Island, the Exuma and several others. Most romance seekers set their sights on Paradise Island, where an exquisite selection of resorts is available, with myriad activities, duty-free shopping, casinos, and fine dining. Visit **www.bahamas.com** or **www.nassauparadiseisland.com** for additional information.

# ASK THE EXPERTS

**We're considering Puerto Rico for our honeymoon, but we're worried because neither of us speaks Spanish.**

Don't worry. Many people living in Puerto Rico, especially those working at the resorts, are bilingual. You'll be able to communicate without a problem.

**The U.S. Virgin Islands look great for a honeymoon. Where should we stay?**

If it's within your budget, don't miss The Ritz-Carlton St. Thomas. This jewel combines European elegance and Mediterranean accents with a Caribbean motif. The property is located on 15 acres of waterfront, bestowing many guest-room balconies with a view of the Caribbean Sea and St. Johns'. Rounding out this resort is a swimming pool, 18-hole golf course, half a mile of calm beach area with an aquatic center offering scuba diving and snorkeling, a fitness center, tennis courts, a 53-foot catamaran, and several restaurants (**www.ritzcarlton.com**, 800-241-3333). If the Ritz is out of your budget, consider the lovely Marriott Beach Resorts: Frenchman's Reef and Morning Star.

**We've narrowed down our honeymoon location to Paradise Island in the Bahamas. Which resorts should we consider?**

Investigate the following to see if they meet your requirements: Atlantis (**www.atlantis.com**, 888-528-7155), Nassau Marriott Resort & Crystal Palace Casino (**www.crystalpalaceresort.com**, 800-222-7466), Ocean Club (**www.oceanclub.com**, 800-321-3000), Radisson Cable Beach Resort (**www.radissoncablebeach.com**, 800-333-3333), Sandals Royal Bahamian Resort and Spa (**www.sandals.com**, 888-SANDALS), and SuperClubs Breezes (**www.superclubs.com**, 877-GO-SUPER).

# beachy keen

## Bermuda, Jamaica, and Aruba

*W*hile Bermuda, Jamaica, and Aruba are not close to one another on the map, they do share one thing in common: exquisite natural beauty. Sail 570 miles southeast of Cape Hatteras, North Carolina, and you'll discover Bermuda. When you arrive, you'll immediately smell the sweet scent of flowers. The island is in bloom almost year-round. You'll find golfing, fishing, sailing, swimming, diving, and horseback riding. The resorts and bed-and-breakfasts reflect British ideals, so you can indulge in five-course meals, spa treatments, and horse-drawn carriage rides. (**www.bermudatourism.com**, 800-BERMUDA).

Jamaica is one of the most popular honeymoon spots because it's always sunny and warm, the people are friendly, the beaches are stunning, and all-inclusive resorts rule. There are several distinct areas of this large island: Kingston, Montego Bay, Ocho Rios and Runaway Bay, Negril, Port Antonio, and South Coast. To learn about the unique personality of each district, contact The Jamaica Tourist Board (**www.jamaicatravel.com**, 800-233-4JTB).

Aruba is a small island—about 20 miles long and 6 miles wide—located in the heart of the southern Caribbean, just 15 miles north of Venezuela. It's outside the hurricane belt, and the weather is lovely all year, so it's heaven for sunbathers, divers, fishermen, and golfers. In the evening, you can relax at a fine restaurant or visit one of the casinos (**www.aruba.com**, 800-TO-ARUBA).

# ASK THE EXPERTS

**We've heard that Bermuda is beautiful, but dining out there can be very expensive.**

Many hotels and resorts offer dining plans, which can be worth the money if you plan to stay on the property most of the time. You may also elect to stay in a cottage or apartment with kitchen facilities so that you can cook one or more of your meals each day and save a little money.

**Any tips on avoiding hurricane season?**

Hurricane season is July through October. If you're concerned about booking a trip during this time period, consider purchasing trip insurance (see page 177). Some resorts, such as the Sandals and Beaches properties, actually offer a hurricane guarantee. If hurricane-force winds hit a Sandals or Beaches resort while you're a guest, they will offer you a free replacement vacation.

**We enjoy vacation spots with wild nightlife. Will we find enough in Aruba to keep us busy for an entire week?**

Aruba does have nightclubs and casinos, but the activity level is not as high as on, say, San Juan, Puerto Rico, or Nassau in the Bahamas. Those are better bets if you're party-all-night types.

# international intrigue

## Paris, London, and Venice

*I*f you plan on honeymooning overseas, then the world is truly your oyster. Consider Paris, London, and Venice—three of the most beautiful cities in Europe. Only one word of caution: Visit one city during your honeymoon. Save a whirlwind tour of Europe's capitals for an anniversary.

Paris, the City of Light, is one of the most romantic destinations in the world. There are four main reasons to honeymoon here: monuments, art museums, shopping, and gourmet restaurants. As two lovers in search of romance, don't miss the Louvre art

museum, the Arc de Triomphe, Notre Dame de Paris, Basilique du Sacre Coeur, Versailles, and, of course, the Eiffel Tower. To learn more about this French connection, visit **www.paris-touristoffice.com**.

A visit to London is a great way to decompress. You'll find friendly people, world-class theater, art museums, an enthusiastic nightlife, and, despite what you may have heard, fine dining. You'll want to see Westminster Abbey, the Tower of London, Piccadilly Circus, London Bridge, Big Ben, Covent Garden and the Museum of London. For more information, contact the British Tourist Authority (**www.visitbritain.com**, 800-462-2748).

Venice is actually a group of 118 small islands connected via a vast network of bridges. Due to this unique arrangement, travel in Venice is done on foot or by boat. Amazing sights include the Basilica di San Marco, the Palazzo Ducale and the Grand Canal. And no honeymooning couple can leave the city without taking a romantic moonlit gondola ride (**www.itwg.com/en_venezia.asp**).

# ASK THE EXPERTS

**We'd like to purchase a package tour to Paris. Where should we look?**

Airline packages are often a good place to start. Consider Air France Holidays (**www.airfranceholidays.com**, 800-2-FRANCE), Delta Vacations (**www.deltavacations.com**, 800-654-6559), or Continental Airlines Vacations (**http://continental.coolvacations.com**).

**We've heard about a famous open-air Shakespearean theater in London. Where can we get more information?**

You're referring to Shakespeare's Globe Theatre on the south bank of the River Thames. It opened in 1997 and is a reconstruction of the Globe Theatre of 1599. Performances take place from the end of May through September. For tickets, call the 24-hour box office at 011-44-20-7401-9919 or write to Shakespeare's Globe Theatre, New Globe Walk, Bankside, London, England, SE1 9DR.

# out of the ordinary

## Bali and Down Under

For those seeking something different on their honeymoon, look no farther than Bali and Australia. This trip is especially ideal if you're marrying in winter because it's summer down there.

Bali, in Indonesia, is northwest of Australia and southeast of Thailand. Bali's culture is intertwined with its religion, and some of the country's customs—such as the music of the gamelan (a flute, stringed instruments, xylophone, drums, and gongs)—are intoxicating. Despite the small size of the island, you'll find more than 10,000 temples to visit. While the locals revere their traditions, they also welcome visitors. And you'll have no trouble finding a resort on the beach. To learn more, visit **www.tourismindonesia.com**.

While Australia shares the same general locale as Bali, the culture is much more Western. The unusual flora and fauna make Australia a wonderful destination despite the lengthy air travel. Divers shouldn't miss the Great Barrier Reef, which stretches from Brisbane north to Papua New Guinea. Composed of billions of coral entities, it's 1,200 miles long and 50 miles wide. While exploring this area, it's best to stay on one of the Barrier islands. Then head back to Sydney or Melbourne for a taste of an Australian city. For more information, visit **www.australia.com**.

Balinese dancer

# ASK THE EXPERTS

**Many of the hotels in Bali seem somewhat rustic. Are they up to Western standards?**

Bali is home to many different types of accommodations, and many are not what you'd expect. If you are seeking a luxurious getaway, be sure to book a resort that offers the amenities that are important to you. Work with a travel agent who specializes in Indonesian travel.

**We're taking a three-week honeymoon to Australia and Bali. What are some good books to read about these destinations?**

**Insight Guide Bali** by Garrett Kam

**Lonely Planet Bali & Lombok** by James Lyon

**The Rough Guide Bali & Lombok**
by Lesley Reader and Lucy Ridout

**Diving Bali: The Underwater Jewel of Southeast Asia**
by David Pickell and Wally Siagian

**Fodor's 2003 Australia**

**Frommer's Australia** by Natalie Kruger, Marc Llewellyn, and Lee Mylne

**Lonely Planet Australia** by Denis O'Byrne

**The Rough Guide to Australia** by Margo Daly

# now what do I do?

## Answers to common questions

### How do we get passports?

For all the details, go to the U.S. State Department's Web site (**http://travel.state.gov/passport_services.html**). If you've never applied for a passport before, you'll need to go to the office in person. You can get the appropriate forms at the above-mentioned Web site, from the National Passport Information Center (900-225-5674), or by visiting your local passport agency. The process usually takes six to eight weeks, but it can be expedited—for a higher price—for those in a hurry.

### What's a visa, and will we need one for our honeymoon trip?

A visa is an endorsement, or stamp, placed by officials of a foreign country on a U.S. passport allowing the bearer to visit that foreign country for a set number of days or weeks. Ask your travel agent or airline if a visa is required for your destination. If it is, obtain a visa application from the appropriate foreign consular representative in your state a few weeks before your trip. A list of consular addresses can be found at **www.state.gov**. You'll need to fill out the paperwork and return it with the appropriate documentation. Once the visa is approved, you'll receive confirmation paperwork and will get a visa stamp in your passport when you arrive in your destination country.

### What should we pack in our honeymoon survival kit?

Make sure you carry proper identification (passports, driver's licenses, birth certificates) and travel documents (airline tickets, hotel confirmation numbers) in your purse or carry-on bag. Next, keep any prescription medications, along with the prescriptions themselves, in your carry-on. Also toss in over-the-counter medications such as cold and sinus pills, antacids, and diarrhea medication.

### How much does the average honeymoon cost?

The average honeymoon, which averages nine days, costs $3,500. A good rule of thumb: Never spend more than you can afford to but don't be afraid to splurge if it means stretching your budget only a bit.

**A lot of the resorts we're considering offer three room categories: standard, deluxe, and concierge. What does concierge mean?**

Technically, a **concierge** is a resort or hotel employee who caters personally to guests. He makes dining reservations, secures tennis times, procures tickets to special events, and more. His services are available to all guests. Concierge accommodations are something quite different. In general, these lodgings are a deluxe room or suite on a private floor of the hotel. On this private concierge floor, you'll find a concierge lounge with daily complimentary food and beverage services: breakfast in the morning, a light lunch in the afternoon, midday snacks, wine and cheese before dinner, and evening cordials and desserts. A concierge is usually stationed in the lounge to answer your questions and to assist with your needs. Concierge accomodations are usually more expensive than deluxe.

# NOW WHERE DO I GO?!

**CONTACTS**

Concierge.com

Expedia.com

Fodors.com

Frommers.com

**VACATION PACKAGES FROM AIRLINES**

Air France Holidays
**www.airfranceholidays.com**
800-2-FRANCE

Alitalia
**www.alitaliausa.com/vacations**

American Airlines Vacation
**www.aavacations.com**, 800-321-2121

Continental Airlines Vacations
**http://continental.coolvacations.com**

Delta Vacations
**www.deltavacations.com**, 800-654-6559

United Vacations
**www.unitedvacations.com**, 888-854-3899

**BOOKS**

**Checklist for a Perfect Honeymoon**
by Suzanne Rodriguez-Hunter

**The Good Honeymoon Guide: Includes Where to Get Married Abroad**
by Lucy Hone

**100 Best Romantic Resorts of the World**
by Katharine D. Dyson

**Romantic Wedding Destinations: Guide to Wedding & Honeymoon Getaways Around the World**
by Jackie Carrington

# glossary

**Annulment:** A judicial pronouncement declaring a marriage invalid.

**Bill on consumption:** This means the bar bill at your reception will be tallied according to how many drinks of what type were ordered and served. You will be billed per drink.

**Blackout dates:** Dates on which certain travel packages and deals are not valid. These dates include holidays, as well as a few days before and after them.

**Blended family:** A family of mixed religious, ethnic, or racial backgrounds.

**Bouquet toss:** A tradition in which the bride tosses her bouquet toward all the single women at the reception. Whoever catches the bouquet is said to be the next to marry.

**Budget:** The total amount you plan to spend on all aspects of your wedding.

**Bustle:** Most wedding-gown trains can be "bustled" for the reception. This means that the length of the train is gathered up and attached to hidden hooks and buttons on the back of the dress—thus shortening it. This makes it easier for the bride to dance and move about the reception without tripping on her train.

**Buttercream:** A type of frosting that is often used for wedding cakes. It is light and creamy with a buttery flavor.

**Cash bar:** This indicates that your guests will pay for their own drinks at the bar at your reception.

**Caterer:** The company providing food, and sometimes bar service, for your reception.

**Chuppah:** A canopy that can be made of cloth or flowers. At Jewish weddings, the bridal party stands under the covering during the ceremony. It symbolizes the new home the couple is about to enter as man and wife.

**Civil ceremony:** A ceremony devoid of religious undertones that is presided over by a justice of the peace.

**Couture:** A French word used to denote original styles, of the highest quality tailoring and made of expensive fabrics.

**Destination wedding:** A wedding which takes place in a location that is neither the home of the bride nor the groom. Destination weddings may take place on tropical islands, at country inns, or at theme parks.

**Elope:** To run away secretly with the intention of getting married.

**Engaged:** Two people who have pledged to get married.

**Eucharist:** Sharing of bread and wine during the ceremony that symbolizes the body and blood of Jesus Christ and the couple's commitment to God.

**Exchange of rings:** The point at which the bride and groom place a wedding band on each other's ring finger.

**Garter toss:** During the reception, the bride sits on a chair in the middle of the room and allows her new husband to slip the garter off her leg. He then throws it to the pack of single male guests. Whoever catches the garter is supposedly the next to get married.

**Gift registry:** When a couple gets engaged, they often register for gifts at a local department store or online catalog. The registry lists the gift items the couple would like to receive.

**Intercession:** A short prayer after the exchange of rings and/or lighting of the unity candle.

**Interfaith marriage:** A marriage involving persons of different religious faiths.

**Intimate wedding:** A small, low-key wedding with only a handful of guests or just the bride, groom, maid of honor, and best man present.

**Invocation:** A prayer at the beginning of a wedding ceremony.

**Ketubah:** A marriage contract that is signed at Jewish wedding ceremonies.

**Laser printing:** Use of an electrostatic charge to transfer the image onto the paper.

**Marriage license:** A document issued by the state that certifies that you are legally free to marry.

**Mass:** See Eucharist.

**Medium format camera:** Medium format cameras use film that results in a negative that is 6.5cm wide. This is larger than the standard 35mm negative. The larger the negative, the better the color saturation will be. Enlargements will be grain-free.

**Nondenominational ceremony:** Representing no particular religious organization or affiliation during the ceremony.

**Offset lithography:** Offset printing starts with a flexible plate that contains your invitation wording. It is inked and the image is transferred to paper.

**Officiant:** A person who presides over a wedding ceremony.

**Open bar:** This means you pay for all drinks consumed at your reception. Your guests will have unlimited access to the bar.

**Photojournalism:** Wedding photojournalism is the art of capturing the wedding as it happens, rather than creating it via posed shots.

**Pre-Cana:** Premaritial counseling that is required of all couples who wish to be married in the Catholic Church.

**Prenuptial agreement:** A legal contract that spells out the rights of each person in regard to the property of the other in the event of divorce, separation, or death.

**Processional:** The musical prelude to which the official wedding party walks down the aisle.

**Receiving line:** A line formed by the wedding party after the ceremony or right before the reception starts. Your guests will approach the receiving line so each member of the wedding party can greet them individually.

**Recessional:** The order of the wedding party leaving the ceremony.

**Rolled fondant:** A sturdy, paste-like frosting that is used to cover elaborate wedding cakes.

**Sacred music:** Songs that can be played in a house of worship.

**Save-the-date letter:** An announcement of your upcoming wedding that goes to your guest list before the actual invitations are sent out. Send a save-the-date letter if you are hosting a destination wedding and your guests need time to make travel plans, or if your wedding date falls on a popular holiday or vacation period.

**Shoulder season:** The dates in between peak and low season.

**Stationer:** A company that specializes in working with invitation manufacturers. You will order your wedding announcements, invitations, and some paper products (such as napkins and cake boxes) from a stationer.

**Themed wedding:** An event that captures a certain theme such as Cinderella's Ball, Winter Wonderland, or Spring Garden.

**Thermography:** A method of printing wedding invitations using ink that contains a special powder. When heated, the ink raises a bit and becomes shiny.

**Unity candle:** A unity candle consists of one large candle in the center of a floral arrangement, with two taper candles on either side. The mothers light the tapers. This symbolizes the two families that have come together on this special day. The bride and groom take the tapers and light the center candle together.

**Vows:** Promises you and your fiancé make to each other to affirm your love, respect, and eternal bond.

**Wedding coordinator:** A person hired to make sure your wedding day runs smoothly.

**Wedding Party:** Those members who play an active role in your wedding. These include the maid of honor, best man, bridesmaids, groomsmen (ushers), flower girl(s), ring bearer, and your parents.

# index

# THE AUTHOR: UP CLOSE

**Andrea Rotondo Hospidor** has written extensively about weddings and marriage for numerous magazines. She is a destination wedding expert and is on the Advisory Council for Disney's Fairy Tale Weddings and Honeymoons division.

She would like to thank the following people for their help in preparing this book: Rebecca Grinnals of Engaging Concepts, everyone at Disney's Fairy Tale Weddings department, Shelley Geery of Impressions, Liz Lynch of Once Upon a Time Bridals, all the Disneymooners, and TPATH.

**Barbara J. Morgan**  Publisher, Silver Lining Books

**Barnes & Noble Basics**™

**Barb Chintz**  Editorial Director

**Leonard Vigliarolo**  Design Director

**Barnes & Noble Basics**™ *Getting Married*

**Giulia Zarr**  Editor

**Ann Stewart**  Picture Research

**Emily Seese**  Editorial Assistant

**Della R. Mancuso**  Production Manager